# HONEY, I SHRUNK THE FARM

## BY
## DR. VAL FARMER

# HONEY, I SHRUNK THE FARM

Author - Dr. Val Farmer
Publisher - McCleery & Sons Publishing

International Standard Book Number: 0-9700624-3-5
Printed in the United States of America

# PREFACE

For the 25 years I've lived in North and South Dakota , I've stood in awe of the lives and values of rural families. This has been a unique, different experience. I've tried to understand why and I'm still trying. I've written about unique themes - stories and lives playing themselves out in agricultural communities nationally but especially in the northern plains and prairie provinces.

I've learned first hand from rural people who have shared their pain, their worries, their joy, their hopes and their dreams with me. I've been a privileged witness and story teller of a special people in special circumstances.

The landscape is unique. It is vast, open, empty - so different from the tree-lined highways of the moisture-blest east and south. Here you see something besides trees, cars, people and concrete. Here you can see a horizon, a big sky, a starlit night, empty roads, cultivated land and land that resists human imprint.

The climate is unique. Nature has to be respected. I've skidded off the interstate on black ice. Once I foolishly drove at night in eastern South Dakota when the wind chill was close to 100 below zero. A person exposed to the elements could have frozen to death within 10 minutes. What about blizzards, tornadoes, thunderstorms and deer on highways? The slightest miscalculation can be fatal.

Farmers and ranchers have always been dependent upon the weather, and so have the rural communities and cities that service them. Some years the land seemed like it would dry up and blow away. Other years wet fields and flooding conditions had farmers holding their breath about getting into their fields. There have been hailstorms, killer frosts, prairie fires and burning forests. Just when you think you've seen it all, you haven't.

This is a fragile land. So much depends on timely rains. Sometimes it hits just right. Kathleen Norris captures the feeling in her book, "Dakota: A Spiritual Geography." "After a long drought I have realized that a long soaking rain in spring or fall, a straight -down-falling rain, a gentle splashing rain is more than a blessing. It is a miracle."

The saving grace is that Dakotans and northern plains people understand and prepare for adversity. We have a concept of bad years and dig in a little deeper. We hang in there for "next year." This is "next year" country.

When crops and livestock are stressed, humans are stressed. When biology fails, humans sometime fail. This is a land of hidden and not so hidden dependencies. Our vulnerabilities are close to the surface and nature occasionally shatters our illusions of control.

During the mid-80s it wasn't a weather crisis but a debt crisis brought on by human policies and error. Inflation and lending practices based on inflation came back to haunt the agricultural economy. Faith and trust were shattered by institutions and people. The independent farmer was more dependent than he dreamed. For some, the healing process from those rude and dark days rolls on.

In the late 90s, it was an Asian economic downturn, weather problems, globalization and the inexorable march of technology that helped produce record low prices.

Why farm or ranch? What accounts for the tenacity and perseverance of farmers and ranchers? What is the allure of an occupation that depends on application of biological knowledge? Why be subject to all the unpredictability of biology, disease, weather and uncertain market prices?

Economics is a part of it. Successful farmers and ranchers are able to enjoy good profits. It is an occupation from which you can make a comfortable living. It is a secret not talked about much, but a reality that sustains many hopes and dreams.

A treasure trove of knowledge and experience on the land is stored and passed on to the next generation. The farm itself is a heritage, a gift passed from generation to generation. Victories come by attention to detail. Small victories lead to large victories. Each day is different. Each day can be a challenge. There is the thrill of being one's own boss in an honorable profession that sustains life for so many others.

Occasionally time stands still. Meeting the challenge of the moment becomes the most important thing, despite how long it takes. Crops need to be nurtured. Livestock need attention. We grow to love what we serve. It is easy to love the farm. Work is love made visible.

**This attachment isn't just about money and work.** Add to the mix all the lifestyle considerations that make farming satisfying. Rural people like their neighbors, communities and close relatives. The human face of agriculture is full of joy, faith and rewarding human relationships. It is an artful blend of work, love, family and community life. It is a place where it is easy to love others.

The farm is good for children, both for being around nature and taking meaningful responsibility. Husbands and wives can enjoy true partnerships in business and in companionship. Nature is just outside the door. And the door is a long way from the neighbor's door.

Who among those who have lived here hasn't thrilled to a mighty wind, the awesome power of a blizzard, the paralyzing fury of which causes us to retreat to our homes and enjoy our impotence with our family? Even nature gone violently awry has a spiritual and humbling quality.

Who among those who have lived here hasn't felt a spiritual relationship with the Creator because of this closeness to nature? Prayer might come a little easier to those whose livelihood depends on what the heavens may bring.

Can you see the love? Can you feel the pain when that love is not requited? I can.

These are high stress, dangerous and physically demanding occupations. The work hours are incredibly long. The risks are great. These are high-stake, gambling occupations.

It is about families. Generations work together and build a heritage. A treasure trove of knowledge and experience about the land is stored and passed on to the next generation.

It is about creation and nurturing young life. It is about independence and tests of management. Victories come by attention to detail. Small victories lead to large victories. Each day is different. Each day can be a challenge.

It is about raising children in a family business in which they can contribute. It is about community - friends and neighbors that know and care for each other. It is about small towns and hometowns. It is about dependence on God and on each other.

The human face of the plains is full of joy, faith and rewarding human relationships. It is an artful blend of work, love, family, belief and community life. Everyone needs each other to survive. In her book, "Dakota, A Spiritual Geography," Kathleen Norris observes, "The Plains are not forgiving. Anything that is shallow - the easy optimism of the homesteader; the false hope that denies geography, climate, history; the tree whose roots don't reach ground water - will dry up and blow away." We are still here.

I wrote a booklet, "The Rural Stress Survival Guide", after the flooding conditions of 1993. This book, "Honey, I Shrunk the Farm", is a compilation of columns I wrote since the publication of that booklet. The vast majority of topics on farm stress and coping in this book were written during and after the horrific winter of 1996-97 on the Northern Plains and the subsequent down years in agriculture from 1998 through the present.

My office was again filled with farmers and farm couples trying to make sense of their lives and deal with the challenges they faced. I received letters from readers of my syndicated column telling their perspective and stories about how the farm crisis was affecting them. I've included parts of their letters in this book. I've kept the anonymity of the authors and in a few cases, where necessary, have disguised a few key facts to insure their privacy.

I've experienced a part of the history of agriculture. Where helpful, I refer to the date and circumstances under which the original article or letter occurred. The current downturn in the farm economy and the impact it has on family farmers rivals or surpasses the difficult farm crisis years of the mid-80s.

I didn't think I would have a second round of writing about farm stress in my lifetime. Here we are again and, unhappily, the ending to this crisis is not over. The bins are again busting. Prices dip to new historical lows and the shake out of smaller and mid-size family farmers continues. I hope this book will comfort and give clarity to those who find themselves in the path of these bewildering events.

# INTRODUCTION

Dr. Val Farmer has embraced the plight of today's farm families like no other figure on the American scene. In newspaper columns and radio appearances, from meeting halls to one-on-one counseling sessions, he speaks to the hearts of those who suffer. And suffer they do, the stewards of our great agricultural expanse – to the limits of endurance. Machinery goes on the auction block. Banks foreclose. The nation appears indifferent to the loss of a once honored way of life: family farming.

Seldom do we see authors or pundits actually help save lives, whatever lofty causes they lay claim to – but I have witnessed this rare phenomenon. The night was black, with the North Dakota wind so cold it took your breath away. Rural families had gathered on a winter night (in the wake of the disastrous floods and ice storms of 1997) to hear Dr. Farmer's words of hope. I was at the meeting.

After a question and answer period, one of the farmers quietly asked me for my card. The next day, I received a call from this same man, who asked if I was connected to Dr. Farmer, or knew whether he was available for a crisis intervention. A neighboring farmer, the man told me, was contemplating suicide. Within minutes of my contacting Dr. Farmer's office at Meritcare in Fargo, North Dakota, the despairing farmer was reached and told to hold on... that help was on the way. Dr. Val Farmer's friendly persuasion prevailed, and the troubled farmer chose life over death.

Yes, it's pretty dramatic stuff. But not unusual for a man who has touched the lives of literally thousands of rural folks plagued by today's ailing farm economy. This book, the first in the Rural Crisis Survival Series published by McCleery and Sons, may indeed help save lives too. Farm managers who face the loss of their livelihoods, who feel in their hearts that they have let down their forefathers by letting go of a lifestyle, deserve to know they are NOT alone. "Honey, I Shrunk the Farm" is a first step in the healing process. It belongs alongside of Willie Nelson's FarmAid concerts as a prime source of reassurance for rural Americans, who rightly should be viewed as national treasure.

Steve Tweed
Editor
McCleery and Sons Publishing

# TABLE OF CONTENTS

**Chapter one:**

FARM ECONOMICS

Who Will Farm The Land? ............................................... 1

Hunkering Down ................................................. 4

Rural Outlook Not Good .................................... 6

Is There Really An Export Market? ......................... 8

**Chapter two:**

UNDERSTANDING THE FARM CRISIS

Why Farmers Are So Emotional About Farming ............ 13

How Farmers Handle Stress ............................. 16

Observations On The Farm Crisis .................... 18

Farmers Cope With Another Wet Spring .......... 20

Some Times Are Tougher Than Others ........... 22

A Winter To Remember ................................ 25

Stress On The Farm ..................................... 28

How Rural Couples React To Economic Pressures ......... 30

When Debt Comes In the Door,

    Love Goes Out The Window ..................... 32

Film Shows Struggle Of Farm Families ......... 35

All This Milking Is Killing Me ....................... 37

Reations To Letter From Trapped Dairyman ............. 39

The Most Vulnerable Farmers ..................... 42

Why People Attempt Suicide ...................... 45

**Chapter three:**

HOW TO COPE WITH HARD TIMES

Dr. Farmer's Best Advice On The Farm Crisis ............. 49

Why Some Farmers Cope Better Than Others ............ 54

How Thoughts And Emotions Are Connected ........... 57

Where There Is A Will, There Is A Way ......... 59

Explaining Hardships Helps Heal The Teller .................. 62
Taking Control Over Our Lives ......................... 64
Humor Vital As Coping Tool ............................ 67
Farm Crisis Has A Silver Lining ....................... 70
Which Is It? Go To Plan B Or Get A Grip? ..................... 72
Honey, I Shrunk The Farm ............................... 75
When All Else Fails, Lighten Up ...................... 78

**Chapter four:**

FAMILIES GOING THROUGH IT TOGETHER

Farm Women React To Financial Stress ........................ 81
Cowboys Don't Cry And They Don't Talk Much Either .. 83
Marital Support During A Time Of Crisis ....................... 86
Dealing With Differences During A Time Of Crisis ........ 89
Off Farm Work Poses Marital Problems ........................ 91
Two Off-Farm Jobs: Are They Worth It? ...................... 94
How To Help Children During Hard Times ................... 96
How Children Learn To Bounce Back ........................... 99
Youth Asks Questions About Farm Crisis ..................... 101
Making Holiday Traditions On A Low Budget ............. 105

**Chapter five:**

DEALING WITH DEBT

Is Family Farming That Special? ..................... 109
Four Flaws That Get Farmers Into Trouble ................... 112
Ag Financial Counselors Advice: Start Early, Get Help 114
Farmers And Lenders: Yikes! Now What Do We Do? ... 117
Getting Along With Your Lender ....................... 120
Breaking Through Denial During Hard Times ............. 122
Avoid Foreclosure At All Costs ...................... 125
A Loan Officer Replies ............................... 128
Banking 101 And The Foreclosure Issue ...................... 131
Should We Go Through Mediation? ............................. 133

Was It Fair? ........................................................ 140
How To Stop Feeling Like A Victim .......................... 143

**Chapter six:**
GOING FOR HELP, HELPING OTHERS
What Are The Facts About Suicide ........................... 147
When You Suspect Suicidal Thoughts ....................... 150
Help Is Available For Depression ............................. 153
Going To Counseling Is Hard But Helpful ................. 156
Soothing Helps Trauma Victims .............................. 158
Helping Farm Families In Crisis .............................. 160
Helping Others Find Meaning In Crisis ..................... 163

**Chapter seven:**
TRANSITIONS OUT OF FARMING
Out Of Bad Can Come Good .................................... 167
A New, Better Life ................................................ 169
Life After Farming Can Have A Soft Landing ............. 172
Helping Farmers Make A Transition ......................... 177
Decision To Quit Agriculture Made Thoughtfully ........ 180
Moving? Don't Forget The Kids ............................... 182
From The Farm To College ..................................... 185
What Good Is A Farm? ........................................... 187
Two Poems From The Heartland ............................... 190

# ACKNOWLEDGMENTS

I want to take this opportunity to express my appreciation to the many people who contributed to what you are about to read.

To my wife, Darlene, who doubles as an editor and critic: Thank you for your unerring sense of judgement. The truth is sometimes hard to bear. I trust your insight and honesty. Thank you for not letting me get by without giving my best. None of this would have been possible without your support. I am glad I listen to you.

To Trista, my daughter, and her husband, Darin: Thanks for the editing support, the development of www.valfarmer.com and all the other ways you have helped.

To the rest of my children, Tara, Tassa, Tally, Tawny, Tyler and Trace: Thanks for putting up with a Dad who is not perfect. Your happiness in life is my fondest desire. The rising generation takes our place and gives back to us in ways we didn't dream.

To Dixie Davis of the Preston Connection: Thanks for lifting a load, for handling the business end of our enterprise, for your thorough editing and for the little things you notice and do. You have relieved many burdens.

To my colleagues, Ken Root and Rustin Hamilton, at AgriTalk: Your trust in me and our working relationships is a pleasure. It didn't take long for me to understand how radio is as important a vehicle for doing good as the printed word. You have indeed given rural America a voice.

To the rural people I've met along the journey of life: I am proud to tell your story. Thank you for sharing your hearts with me.

To the people I've seen in counseling: Thanks for your trust. You are special. You have the courage to improve your lives, no matter what it takes. Your struggles give life to my writing.

To the MeritCare Foundation: Thanks for recognizing the struggles of farm families as a legitimate need and as a part of your mission. Your resources have helped many lives.

To Steve Tweed and Hap McCleery of McCleery & Sons Publishing: Thanks to you for your commitment to rural people, families and community life. You are proof capitalism has a heart. You can take pleasure in knowing that these ideas are in the hands of people who have a real need for them. You had the vision for this book and made it happen.

*CHAPTER ONE*

# FARM ECONOMICS

## Who Will Farm The Land?

Who will farm the land? This is not an idle question. It is of great concern to agriculture families whose commitments run deep. Their goals include seeing their children staying on the family farm.

Who will be tomorrow's farmers? I posed this question to Mike Boehlje, Professor of Agricultural Economics at Purdue University. He talked about the skills and strategies farmers need to be successful.

- **The low cost producer.** Producers can compete by increasing their production while keeping their costs low. Their basic management strategy is using technology and large scale production methods to cut costs wherever they can. They will take the price risks of the global marketplace. They will farm more efficiently and stay competitive with better methods. Boehlje calls this trend the industrialization of agriculture.

- **The farmer who produces a value-added product.** These are the producers who compete by producing a specialized or value-added product integrated into the needs of the food processor, distributor and consumer. Marketing is the name of the game. To compete, farmers will need to gain marketing clout through direct contracting, buying or marketing cooperatives, alliances and networks.

The shift to being a specialty producer who commands premiums in the marketplace requires an awareness of technological advances. They will need negotiation and relationship building skills with business partners.

• **The low input farmer.** There is a small but persistent niche for low input sustainable agriculture fueled by environmental and consumer demands. These operations will be more labor intensive and require a total systems approach to maximizing productivity on the farm. Mainstream conventional farmers will adopt many of these methods. This industry depends on building up a marketing infrastructure to promote and distribute their specialized and certified products.

• **The farmer who diversifies.** Farmers who diversify their production can withstand low prices in a particular enterprise. Many farmers diversify by adding on-farm businesses to their main farming business.

• **The farmer with financial skills.** Financial management and record keeping are a key to farming no matter what course of action a farmer chooses. Survival depends on having enough liquid working capital to cushion the down times or to grow when opportunities exist.

Stress causes many families to leave agriculture. People wear out in an occupation that combines high financial risks and hard work with uncertain rewards. When farming works, it really works and when it doesn't, it takes a big toll on mental health and family well-being. Some families recognize this and choose to leave farming for a less stressful way of life. The cost outweighs the benefits.

• **The farmer with an outside income.** Producers can survive in farming by supplementing income from outside sources. Off-farm work helps subsidize the farm. This is a high stress strategy in terms of personal time allocation and compromises with lifestyle. Yet many farm families will maintain their foothold in agriculture by persistent effort and sacrifices. Boehlje points out that outside investors - doctors and lawyers for example - can invest and maintain farms based on their professional incomes.

- **The farmer who survives on equity.** Farmers who have enough equity can survive in spite of not being heavily invested in one of these strategies. It is disheartening though to see a slow attrition of their assets over time.

- **The farmer who does custom farming.** Many older farmers choose to lease or rent their land. This presents opportunities for farmers to farm without needing to invest in land. Custom farming helps farmers with off-farm commitments, retirees and those farmers who choose not to invest in expensive, specialized machinery. Opportunities for custom farming will expand.

- **Well-educated, beginning farmers.** Iowa State University rural sociologist Paul Lasley points out that according to the 1994 Iowa farm Poll, only one-third of those farmers 55 or older plan to keep their land in the family. A fourth of the remainder plan to rent out their land as a part of their retirement.

Two-thirds of the Iowa land will eventually come on the market. Who will farm the land? It will be farmers who expand their operations, outside investors and corporations that see production agriculture as a profitable enterprise. Public policy can play an active role in supporting "beginning farmer" programs that provide low investment systems and networking opportunities to bring young farmers into agriculture.

- **Farmers who have positive family relationships in farming.** The succession and eventual success of the next generation in agriculture depend on relationships within the family as well. Children, particularly boys, who grow up with positive relationships with their fathers, who experience a positive lifestyle on the farm and learn the multiple skills of being a farmer, get farming in their blood. Poor father/son relationships cause young people to choose another way of life.

Eighty-three percent of children of farmers on sustainable farms want to come back to the farm. Only 47 percent of the children of conventional farmers are interested in farming.

Children of full-time farmers are more likely to choose a future in agriculture while children of part-time farmers typically do not. A stressful and hectic lifestyle coupled with marginal prospects for success figure into their choices. Despite obvious difficulties of entering a high risk, high stress occupation, there will be young people with a love for farming who want an opportunity to farm.

Who will rent the farm? It will still be families for the most part but it will be different. It will be tougher. Rewards are there for those who can stay "in the game" or find a way to get in.

# Hunkering Down

I received a letter from a woman expressing how she and her family are coping with the poor farm economy.

Dr. Farmer,

I so enjoy listening to you on AgriTalk. I listen to other people talk and usually think, "Hey, we're not doing too badly," or, "Yeah, I've felt just like that." It's nice, though not always pleasantly so, to realize a lot of us are in the same farming boat.

I honestly don't know how we do what we do. We have been married 31 years, we live on my husband's "home place." We have 2 children age 15 and 13. They are the 4th generation to live here. I don't work off the farm, neither does my husband. We have 360 acres which we either own or are paying on. We rent another 400 acres. We don't live rich but we have everything we NEED and most things we WANT.

We are both high school graduates. We have no hired help. We take a family vacation (though not a long one) each year. We take days off together, usually to go to a larger town to stock up on groceries and eat lunch out. We're home by the time the kids are home from school. We also have kid days when we go to a show or take them shopping.

By the way, we have no outstanding credit card bill, never have. That was the deal made when I got the first one. Most profit goes back into the farm. We seldom buy "new" but what we have is well taken care of. Sure there are things I'd like to do in the house but we don't live in a run-down shack.

We NEED a new patio door. It's been on the "must do" list for 2 years now. With prices the way they are, I'll have the "ceremonial duct tape sealing of the door for the winter" and when we can, we'll replace the door. It's not falling out, it just leaks air - badly. With enough tape, it's fine.

Maybe what I'm trying to say is you CAN live well on a small farm. I don't feel we do without, nor do our children. I don't feel poor, I don't often feel deprived. We live simply and within our means. We have had hard years. We've owed a LOT of money to the bank. We don't have money put away for retirement but we have the land to sell if we need it because we are not encouraging our children to enter this lifestyle. It isn't so much fun anymore but it is what we DO. I don't care to do anything else though somedays you wonder why. But isn't that true with any job? – e-mail via the Internet

# Rural Outlook Not Good

In the spring of 1997, I asked readers to fill out a survey about their well being and happiness. At the end of the survey many rural readers added their comments about how they felt about the rural economy. Here is what they said:

"Environmental issues also determine happiness with our community. Income dissatisfaction due to the amount of return for the number of hours worked. Too little pay! The price of cattle doesn't keep up with the cost hikes.

"In general, very satisfied. With the farm situation, not at all."

"Returned to this area four years ago - never realized the stress of farming when growing up here."

"I feel that as a minority group of Americans, the small farmer is so important to the world, yet we are not given the true support and recognition we need."

"Wheat scab disease and poor prices at the same time destroyed our equity from 1993 to 1997. I am happy with my marriage but it is so hard to make a living at farming. It is very stressful. Through 1992 we had everything paid for. The years 1993 and 1994 ate up all our equity. Since then we're still dealing with disease, poor yields and poor prices. Not a pretty picture."

"As long as the federal government's cheap food policy receives top priority, producers of real wealth (farmer/ranchers, lumbermen, and fishermen) will continue to be squeezed. Families of producers are overwhelmed with the restrictive federal regulations, monopolistic practices of processor conglomerates, dependency on commodity exports to say nothing of the vagaries of weather, plant/animal diseases, insects and economics of hired help. All have a negative impact on the welfare of families/communities."

"Farming is a horrible struggle against the elements because it's always going to rain tomorrow and undone work will cost us thousands. It is not practical that the answer to problems is to take a day off for a picnic with the kids."

"Farm prices are terribly low and expenses extremely high. That makes for a very negative outlook on life."

"I am extremely frustrated with our perennial wheat scab problem and diminished income. Now we are losing 'normal' farmers."

"My wife teaches to make our living. I farm 1100 acres and can't make a living!"

"Most personal life negativism is a direct result of the economic status of American agriculture and the public's attitude."

"Myself and all my farm friends do not wish to get rich, just wish we could break even and continue to live the farm life."

From a small business owner - "I am always amazed at how hard most farm families work. My husband and I work extremely hard to keep our business profitable . . . After 15 years of this, we are not sure where we would or could go if we decided to discontinue our business. I guess we thought we'd be further along at this point in our lives. If it were a more profitable business, we'd never consider leaving."

"I am disappointed in farm prices compared to expenses."

"Farming and ranching aren't so good now. Prices for cattle etc. are too low. Expenses too high."

"We have five kids 22 to 11. Two in college and three in braces. Not good!"

"Community of 100 is too small. Not enough friends here. Many moved. No social opportunities makes me feel isolated, causes tension, stress and depressed feelings!"

"I guess I am a happy person. Good marriage but do not enjoy farm life anymore. My husband loves it."

One reader included a concise summary of the changes she saw in her rural community and farm economy and how it is affecting her family.

"I have worked long and hard for my family, farm and community and was a stay-at-home mom. Now with the farm barely making it and friends moving away or working full time, it seems my having a career would have been a wiser choice both economically and emotionally.

"I would have answered the survey questions much differently ten years ago. Those ten years have seen these changes: Our community has lost the high school, bowling alley and snack bar, legion and little league baseball, grocery and hardware store, 'Women of Today' and other organizations. Many couples are retiring to larger cities and many young people are moving to out-of-state jobs.

"What remains is a bar, cafe, and car dealership with gas and service. There are no health services, but there is a bus service for the elderly. There are three churches. Two are in danger of closing because of low membership, clergy recruiting and money problems.

"Our family has lost: the joy of farming, farm profitability to disease and poor markets, retirement income to keep the farm afloat, marriage satisfaction from fewer social activities and outlets, grown children to far away jobs, good friends to out-migration and good mental health to stress.

"We also have one son who is beginning to get involved in the farming operation. I can foresee lots of problems should he marry and try to find a girl who would be happy living here or if he should have to commute and not live on the land. Also, there is the question, can any of the next generation afford to farm or ranch no matter how good their management skills are? We are hanging onto our sanity by a thread out here on the plains of Dakota!!"

# Is There Really An Export Market?

Since the early 1960s the world's grain production has doubled and livestock production has tripled. Is that adequate for the people in the world? No. About 820 million people lack the food they need to lead healthy and productive lives. About 170 million children are seriously underweight.

These figures were used in the presentation by Per Pinstrup-

Andersen at a joint meeting of the American and Canadian Phyto-pathological Associations in Montreal, Canada, August 1998. Pinstrup-Andersen is the Director General of the International Food Policy Research Institute (IFPRI) in Washington D.C.

Pinstrup-Andersen went on to review projections about world-wide food availability by the year 2020. These projections are based on population trends coupled with economic and political analysis of various countries with regard to food production and consumption.

During the next quarter of a century, the world will likely grow by 80 million people a year to go from 5.5 billion to 7.7 billion in 2020. Ninety-five percent of the growth will be in developing countries. The highest absolute population increase will be in Asia while the highest relative increase will be in Sub-Saharan Africa. The urban population in the developing world will double. This rural/urban migration will lead to the use of more rice, wheat, livestock products, fruits, vegetables and processed foods.

The developing world will drive the increase in the world food demand. Food production in developing countries will not keep pace with demand. An increasing portion of this demand will be met by imports from the developed world.

**People's access to food depends on income.** Incomes are expected to rise the fastest in China and East Asia while Russia and the former eastern block countries will experience the lowest rate of economic growth. Poverty is likely to remain entrenched in South Asia and Latin America while increasing considerably in Sub-Saharan Africa.

As incomes increase, people add meat to their diet. By 2020, developing countries, led by China and East Asia, will increase their net meat imports to 20 times their current levels. Asia will switch from a small net exporter of meat to a large net importer. The per capita demand for meats is projected to increase by 43 percent while per capita demand for cereal grains will increase by only 8 percent. The crisis in the U.S. pork industry in 1997-1998 was the direct result of East Asian economic troubles.

Pinstrup-Andersen presents an interesting path for the development of export markets in the developing world. When the United States and other developed countries share their agricultural research and technology with developing countries, the increase in food self-sufficiency frees up economic growth outside of the ag sector. As a country's general economy and purchasing power improve, the demand for meats, fruits, vegetables and processed foods increase. The country then imports the foods they need to satisfy the rising demand.

Asia's present export market was originally created by the "green" revolution in agriculture because of the application of western technology and innovation. Rapid growth in agriculture efficiency eventually led to food imports.

I asked Pinstrup-Andersen why China will be an attractive export market for agricultural products? He stated that China is a large country with a huge domestic market. They have had sensible agricultural policies and a stable currency. The rising standard of living in China will create a thriving domestic market for agriculture products as well as demands for imported foods.

The Ukraine has been beset by disastrous ag policies that resulted in a 50 percent reduction of their productivity. If the government corrects those policies, then the Ukraine could emerge during the next decade as a major food exporter on the world scene.

**The situation in Russia is chaotic.** The institutions in the countryside are ineffective. There is anarchy and corruption. Pinstrup-Andersen doesn't see Russia emerging as either a large food exporter or large importer during the next twenty years. Russia can't afford to buy the food it needs or would like.

India has put several economic reforms in place that are promising for their economy. However, the future food situation in India is complicated because of religious and cultural restrictions on meat consumption.

North Africa, Sub-Saharan Africa and West Asia will continue to need food aid. The best way to provide food aid is to feed the poor children and elderly who do not have purchasing power. Providing food in the schools is an excellent example of how to do this. Food aid complements local agriculture instead of undercutting and competing against it.

**Long term projections.** Pinstrup-Andersen predicted world prices for grains would remain low for at least two years, then recover to long term stability for the next ten years before being subject to downward pressures again. Long term trends in real food prices are projected to fall slightly. The developed countries have stagnant population growth. Our incomes are not going to rise as dramatically as incomes in the developing world. Our food consumption will not grow at significant levels and will not create appreciable new demand.

Pinstrup-Andersen believes that both the developing world and the developed world need to understand the role and importance of agricultural research and modern technology, including biotechnology. This will play an important part in meeting the food needs of the next two decades. Our investments in the developing world and their economies, especially their agricultural economy, will affect the economic future and health of our own agricultural industry.

*CHAPTER TWO*

# UNDERSTANDING THE FARM CRISIS

# Why Farmers Are So Emotional About Farming

Why is farming different from any other profession? Why do farmers have a harder time adjusting to the loss of their occupation more than others who are given a pink slip or lose a business?

This winter and spring we will hear again about the trauma of farmers leaving agriculture. Others look at the current prices and wonder how long they can hang on. Routinely, farmers face uncertain market and weather conditions, high cost of inputs, huge capital investments when expanding, and precious little margin of error.

In any given year there is a significant percentage (10-20 percent) of farmers whose finances are marginal and are close to the edge. Of that group, five percent or so face bankruptcy and foreclosure. The impact is real. Emotions run sky high whether it is 1985, 1993 or 1999.

In one way, the current farm crisis may be worse now than during the farm crisis of the mid-80s. It's price, pure and simple. Government aid will help some this year but won't correct the current glut of farm commodities and depressed markets.

Unlike the mid-80s, there is little media hoopla, little in the way of public sentiment or moral indignation and no common cause to rally the public. But within farm communities there is no shortage of hot topics at the "doom and gloom" cafe - industrial size hog farms, multinational grain companies, Canadian/US trade policies, and the effects of "freedom to farm" legislation. Commiseration helps but doesn't pay the bills.

Here are some reasons why farmers develop such an emotional bond with their profession.

- **Community.** The emotional ties to friends, relatives and community are important in the lives of farm families. This sense of belonging in a small, caring community is a powerful bond and an incentive to stay put.

- **Identity.** The composite skills that go into farming form a basic part of a man's identity. A threat to his status as a farmer or rancher may be perceived as a threat to who he is. The more single-minded or focused a person has been on farming as his exclusive activity, the more vulnerable he is.

- **Love.** Farming involves the care and nurture of living things. Crops and animals have needs. Their well-being depends on the farmer being vigilant and dependable in their care. Under these conditions, an attachment or bonding takes place. It is a moral and honorable profession that produces food for others.

- **Fear.** The socialization to agriculture takes place at young ages with positive parent/child involvement and the teaching of skills. Decisions are made early to farm and to take on the family heritage of farming someday. Some farmers haven't experimented much with anything else in life nor do they believe anything else can be as rewarding. They may underestimate their skills and abilities to be valuable in another part of the economy and don't know what else in life might be enjoyable.

- **Status.** One's status in the community depends on his managerial competence and farm ownership. To have financial problems become public or to lose a farm represents a major lowering of status in his own eyes and community judgment. There are feelings of shame, guilt and failure.

- **Guilt.** The farm is seen as a link or a bond between generations. The failure to keep the "family" farm is perceived as a failure of trust and a violation of a sacred obligation, both to parents and to their children for whom the opportunity to farm "must" be kept alive.
- **Independence.** Farming is an independent business activity. The loss or threat of loss of independence - of working for oneself, of being able to set one's schedule and goals, of having a variety of daily experiences, and of seeing a direct connection between one's labors and rewards - is a significant feat.
- **Lifestyle.** Farmers enjoy the lifestyle of the farm - animals, the closeness to nature, privacy, togetherness with their spouse - and the benefits of raising children in this environment. This is another strong emotional appeal of staying on a farm. To be cooped up by neighbors, concrete, and the congestion of the city violates the sense of space that farmers have come to need. There is also the fear of crime or other influences of the city affecting their children's lives.
- **Failure to seek help.** Farmers are raised with the ethic of solving their own problems. When they become overwhelmed by stress factors beyond their control, they don't feel an inner permission to seek help or express their confusion or pain.

They are afraid to talk about what they are going through with others. This self-imposed isolation deprives them of needed sources of caring and ideas to help them grasp their problem. Being seen in an emotional state and not in control is a threat to their well-being.

Farmers try to cope by working harder and longer, by taking extra work, by using their spouse's off-farm income and by cutting corners. This becomes a special burden of anxiety and depression as they progressively lose ground in their struggle. Marital problems often ensue as each partner fashions their own solution. They also may not be meeting each other's needs or being good parents because of their preoccupied emotional state.

To lose a farm or a ranch is a painful and catastrophic loss. Living with debt is no fun either.

# How Farmers Handle Stress

Beginning in 1998 through the present, we are in the middle of a very difficult time for many farmers and ranchers. Emotions are running high. Prices for their products are at near record lows. Recovery is still over the horizon.

Personality characteristics are more pronounced during hard times. This is apparent to local townspeople, lenders, dealers, creditors, clergy, extension agents, neighbors and family members.

What are farmers or ranchers like? What are their strengths? What are their weaknesses? What kinds of things bug them when they are under stress?

Farmers need to know themselves. Others who work with them need to know where farmers are coming from when they deal with them.

**A typical farmer or rancher personality profile.** Most farmers or ranchers and their spouses would agree with this description of themselves: hard worker, conservative decision-maker, practical, orderly, organized, matter-of-fact, realistic, and dependable.

They feel a strong sense of duty. They value belonging and contributing. They are patient with routine and detail. Success comes because of their ability to be persistent and conscientious.

Farmers and ranchers focus on the "here and now" problems and expect the future to take care of itself. They have a need to be in control and take control of situations when they can. They trust their own judgment and analysis. They are independent almost to a fault.

**Some common weaknesses.** Every set of strengths has its flip side. The same qualities that serve farmers well in their profession can cause problems for themselves and others close to them. Family members of a farmer or rancher see some of these negative characteristics more than they would like.

Farmers and ranchers take a lot for granted. They are known to be critical, sarcastic or impatient. They tend to overwork while having difficulty with leisure and relaxation. They have a hard time expressing love or appreciation. Because they have high standards of performance, they rarely recognize or comment on the efforts of others unless it is truly exceptional.

Farmers and ranchers tend toward a "doom and gloom" appraisal of the future. They are not generally open to new ideas unless they are practical, realistic and related to his or her current mode of operation. They may not see the significance of changing times, outside forces or new developments.

**Farmers under stress.** What kinds of situations are most stressful for farmers or ranchers with this personality profile? They feel stressed out when:

- their plans are blocked, when things don't go right, when there are too many deadlines.
- they are confronted with economic uncertainty, when they lack control, when they can't correct the problem, when the risks are great.
- they don't have enough work to do.
- they are faced with conflict or confrontation, when there are too many people demands, when they feel misunderstood, when they feel let down by someone.
- they don't meet their own expectations, when they make a mistake, when they feel like they've failed.
- they feel lonely or unappreciated.

**So how do other people deal with farmers or ranchers during stressful times?** Here are some things to keep in mind.

- **Be patient.** Give them time to think about the problem. Don't push for an immediate response. Don't humiliate or embarrass them publicly.
- **Be organized.** Present information with facts and figures. Get down to specifics. Work out details in advance. Be logical. Be realistic. Be careful in planning.
- **Teach by concrete example and by "hands on" experience.** Give "how to" advice from trusted authorities.
- **Give appreciation and recognition for their outstanding qualities:** being responsible, industrious, careful, thorough and accurate. These strengths are often overlooked and unappreciated.
- **Don't take criticism personally.** Farmers may think they are stating blunt facts when their remarks are judgmental. There are times when they need to "blow off" steam without being taken too seriously.
- **Be faithful and reliable.** Do your best to understand them, recognize their efforts and follow through with your commitments to them.
- **Reduce risk factors.** Farmers are looking for stability and security - a way of getting back in control.

By reading this, can you get a feeling of why farmers and ranchers feel stressed out when the Ag economy goes in a tailspin?

# Observations On The Farm Crisis

I see a lot of people wearing out in farming. They are just even - staying on the treadmill. The common way of putting it is, "It's no fun any more." They understand it's not working and they would like to get out.

I also meet diehard young people who believe farming is their life. Some of them are third, fourth and fifth-generation farm people who have dirt underneath their fingernails and hold onto farming like dear life. Their commitment to farming ties in with their identity.

The single-minded, workaholic, perfectionist, hard-driving person who has put his life into his work is usually the one who's going to hang on. It's an all-or-nothing proposition. These farmers dearly love what they do and farming gives a lot of meaning to their lives. They are used to being in business and they see working for someone else as a form of slavery. There is a lot of fear about life away from their sheltered, rural community.

On the other hand, the people who are likely to make good adjustments are those who have been college educated or perhaps gone to technical school. They have the confidence that they could succeed in some other walk of life and know it won't be that bad. They feel they have choices. Farming is one way to live a successful life, but it's not the only way. So they are not as wedded to the rural ethic as being pure and virtuous and ennobling with the rest of the world being somehow not as worthy.

There are legitimate concerns about leaving farming. Rural people have life-long ties with family and friends and community. Many are willing to be under-employed or fight to stay in agriculture simply because they don't want to disrupt the ties they have. They haven't experienced starting over in life, making new friends and building new support systems. They would be like a fish out of water. They just can't imagine what it would be like to go somewhere where they don't know anybody, where they have no history with people.

The declining population in rural areas is affecting folks. There is depression that goes with missing people who have left, which means the remaining people are called on to do more and more. There is no surge of enthusiasm or optimism. Instead there is a sense of loss and decline that affects the general mentality of the people who are left.

The keys to successfully adapting to what's going on today in agriculture is a combination of flexibility, good communication, support, religious faith, sense of humor and attitude. People need to be able to move to Plan B or C when Plan A fails.

# Farmers Cope With Another Wet Spring

Here is what I gleaned about a farm situation from my interview with Lowell Nelson, a farmer from Sabin, MN, who was the subject of an ABC "Nightline" farm crisis program.

In our country, in eastern North Dakota and northwestern Minnesota, farmers are being drowned out again, little by little. The water comes on the heels of several wet years that have reduced yields of normally reliable crops. Farmers needed a good start. This has been a tough spring. Things are not going right - again.

**What does a wet spring mean?** A shorter growing season means poorer quality and lower yields. Good yields are crucial when prices are so low. The length of the growing season determines the crop.

For some crops like wheat, hot weather is bad. The cooler it is, the better the crop. Early plantings beat the heat. A late planting followed by an early frost is a terrible combination. That is not a pleasant thought to carry all summer.

"You have sunk a quarter of a million in the ground this spring. Will you get it back?" The most frustrating days are those when you can't do anything.

With a shorter growing season, there is more pressure. When it does dry out, you get out and work hard. It might rain again. Farmers go looking for a dry field and proceed to get stuck. They even know they are out there when they shouldn't be, but they can't help themselves. Work, problems and stress multiply when there is a late spring.

Family life and the schedule go out the window. Marriage is put on hold. Irritation, blame, frustration and temper put a strain on marriage and parenting. Bad weather can eat you alive.

It is not just the farmer but the farmer's wife who is under a strain. Her frustration, her loneliness, her worries, and her discouragement factor into relationship problems. The weather gets to her as well.

It isn't just the amount of rain, but how it comes down. If rain comes down hard there is more trouble. Downpours cause crusting on top of the soil. Standing water washes out and kills seeds. Low spots have a low or no yield. Drowned out spots need to be re-seeded. If you re-seed, then you have two stages of crops in one field. The later crop isn't as good and harvesting is a lot more work. Heavy rains also cause the runoff of fertilizer, insecticides and herbicides into ditches and eventually to rivers.

**What about weeds?** Weeds rob the soil of fertility. The shade of the weeds robs plants of sunshine. Weeds stay green in the fall and plug up the combine. Weed seeds means dockage and discounts. Weeds have moisture and have to be cleaned out or dried before grain is stored. Farmers do not like weeds. The only way to spray wet fields is to hire an airplane which is not "cheap." This means sticking more money into the crop without knowing if you'll get it back.

**So the crop is in. What's next?** A summer hailstorm can wipe everything out in 15 minutes. Farmers live with that fear. They have to carry hail insurance. Yet some years are so bad that farmers pray for a hailstorm. They would be better off with the insurance. Harvest has as much urgency and narrow time frames as does spring planting. Rain during harvest drives down the quality of most crops. It makes harvesting more difficult.

Untimely rains can ruin a hay crop lying on the ground waiting to be picked up. It is one more time when the wrong weather at the wrong time can make you or break you.

Too much wet weather can cause a number of diseases in small grain crops. Wheat "scab" these past several years has caused the demise of farmers more than any other factor. Scab shows up in the fall with nothing in the wheat heads. It is like losing a crop to a hail-storm.

**Weather is the greatest test of a farmer's management.** "We do everything according to the weather, from the spring of the year until it dries up," said Nelson. The weather determines the priorities of the day. His judgment matters. Margins are too thin for bad decisions. That is stress. The only time it doesn't matter is when he is all caught up and that isn't often.

Crops grow and mature. There are beautiful timely rains that makes life so much easier. A farmer gets the weather he wanted. There are tremendous feelings of satisfaction and accomplishment when a farmer knows he's done everything right. Winning the battle with the weather validates his skill.

**So how do farmers cope with the stress of the weather?** They live with it. They have to let go and just react to it. Worrying about it doesn't help. The weather is going to do what the weather is going to do. It takes great *faith* and *optimism* to put seeds in the ground, to *hope* and *pray* for the best, and then *accept* the weather as it comes.

Farmers can handle the stress of farming if they come to terms with the fact that they can do everything right and the weather can still break them. They do not personalize failure. When they win, they feel good. When they lose, the weather got them. That is nothing to be ashamed about. The weather isn't an enemy. It is what it is.

# Some Times Are Tougher Than Others

In the spring of 1997, northern plains cattle producers were fraught with anxiety. They dealt with getting rid of the frozen carcasses of animals caught in deadly blizzards. The weather needed to be warm and dry to not compound calving problems for weak and nutritionally deficient calves.

The toll on the year's feed, snow removal, heating and fuel costs plus the extraordinary wear and tear on equipment needed to be tallied. Obligations had to be met. Cattle prices were inching back up from devastating lows, but hardly enough to make a dent in the bottom line. That winter was a setback of major proportions.

How do farmers and ranchers deal with financial stress? We've been down this road before - drought, spring flooding, poor yields and low prices. The debt crisis of the mid-80s brought tremendous pressure on sound and solidly managed operations. How do producers cope when disaster turns their financial prospects upside down?

**Managing day-to-day responsibilities.** During the winter blizzards, producers could only put one foot in front of the next and get through the day. They did what they had to do to feed and protect their livestock under terrible conditions. Tough winters call for creative management to compensate for problems caused by winter stress.

For hard working farmers and ranchers this plays to their bread and butter strengths - a trouble shooting, hard working, jerry-rigging, practical mind set that deals with the unexpected as it comes. In a pitched battle against the elements they will survive.

**Financial worry.** This is the part that eats people alive. Many operators depend on annual loans to help finance the high expense of agriculture. There is a long time between paydays. Each year is a gamble. Notes come due.

Why go through it? The land is in the family, the work is in the blood and the lifestyle has its special rewards. It takes a special kind of love and mentality to deal with the risks and stress of big time agriculture. The stakes are high and there are so many variables.

Positive and open communication with the lender about their situation may help alleviate concerns or anxiety about the lender's attitude toward this crisis. Others in the same community are in the same boat. Chances are that the lender will have little choice but to work with producers to help them get back on their feet. A working relationship with the lender goes further than avoiding discussion of problems.

**Emotional coping.** Producers get into trouble when they withdraw socially and emotionally and keep problems to themselves. This is tempting because they are tough independent people who believe in solving problems themselves.

A crisis brings out a major test of their flexibility. The traditional answer of working harder isn't sufficient to solve big financial problems and often creates more stress. Farmers have to think and manage their way through a crisis.

Producers need to talk about their emotions. They need to communicate with their spouse and loved ones and to reach out for help they need. Part of successful coping is gathering emotional support, getting good information and having a problem-solving orientation to problems.

**Communications.** During times of high stress and trauma, people need to talk. They need to have a sounding board, feel cared about and get concrete aid and ideas from others. Being angry or irritable drives away support. People should be familiar with symptoms of depression and willing to seek help from clergy, family doctors or counselors.

Their spouses need comfort and kindness more than ever. They want to feel united with their husbands in facing their troubles. What they don't need is to be shut out, be the object of temper outbursts or have the additional worry about their husband's emotional stability.

Likewise children need to understand their parent's stress and be treated with kindness despite their parents' preoccupation. Government bungling and misinformation can be frustrating. Actual disaster relief is a drop in the bucket compared with what is needed.

Still, it is discouraging to deal with paper shuffling when producers feel they have already been kicked around pretty hard by the weather. Displacing anger and blame in that direction won't do much good.

Rely on such positive coping skills as attitude, optimism, self-confidence, religious faith and sense of humor. Timely diversions are also a welcome tool for getting through hard times.

Farmers and ranchers are a tough breed. They can deal with a lot of hardship. Some times are tougher than others.

# A Winter To Remember

The winter of 1996-1997 brought a series of devastating blizzards to the Northern Plains. *"Look kids. See the snow cover the tops of our trees. You'll never see that again."* At least our farmers and ranchers in the Northern Plains hope not. There has never been a winter quite like this one. There have been winters of deep snow. Winters with two or three paralyzing blizzards - the kind where you couldn't move for several days.

Some talk about the winter of '49 when the snow was as deep as you'll ever want to see it. The winter of '66 had its deep snows and rough blizzards, '68 - '69 had huge snowfalls and '77 had tough snow and 60 continuous days of below freezing weather with devastating wind chills. This winter has all of the above. Most people can't remember a tougher winter than this one.

**What is different?** A succession of storms began in early November - one blizzard following on the heels of another. By mid-January, we've had nine and we're still at midwinter. Rural people dig out from one blizzard and the next one comes in. The sequence has been "horrific."

First came a heavy snow over unfrozen ground. The wet fall and early snows left crops unharvested in the fields. The haymovers couldn't get in to move the hay to where it needed to be. This left crops in the field and hay bales in the field.

Then another driving, freezing blizzard came to cover the

first snow fall. A rain and ice storm covered those snows with a thick layer of ice. It was like concrete, a surface you practically needed an ice pick to chop open. Then repeated snows, ice storms, blizzards and deadly wind chills caused major drifts that blocked roads and access to feed, towns and services.

Underneath this mountain of snow is soft muddy ground that prevents equipment from moving. Finding traction is difficult. Ranchers and farmers uncovered some ground with the hope of getting it to freeze over. With the pattern of weekly blizzards, the snow came and blew it over again. The process starts all over. Open roads are sheets of ice.

Snow-covered haystacks have a layer of ice welding them together. Drifts keep ranchers from getting to the feed anyway. Ranchers have a cruel situation - starving cattle that need extra feed to deal with the incessant cold, feed on hand and no way to feed their cattle. Ranchers are running out of accessible feed. This is as painful as it gets.

Death losses are high as the animals are stressed, exhausted and give up. They are blinded and suffocate with ice on their faces. Windbreaks cause major drifting. Cattle can't be moved to safe locations.

**The snow in other winters was workable.** Ranchers could always find a way to feed their cattle after a blizzard. This winter they can't. This winter they can't even get to some of their cattle. Emotionally it rips them apart. One town resident worried, *"How do the cattle keep their sanity in this kind of weather?"* A rancher piped up, *"How about the guys who take care of the cattle? What about their sanity?"*

Pole barns and shop roofs collapse. Metal on metal is brittle and breaks. Diesel jells up. Nothing starts.

Hydraulics won't work. Stress is put on equipment that normally sits idle in the winter. The snow is so tough that major equipment breaks. *"Everything wants to give up."*

Under blizzard conditions people can't get to town to get needed parts. People choose their trips carefully so as not to get stranded in away from their place during the next blizzard. Farmers can't haul their wheat to sell it.

In Hand County, South Dakota, as of mid-January there had been four days of school in the past six weeks that included Christmas vacation. Ranchers feed during the day and clear out snow at night. Power outages are common. Water supplies for the animals are threatened by water pumps breaking down or by electrical outages. Dairymen have to dump milk because they can't move it.

Meanwhile, farmers and ranchers watch wildlife come in to eat feed supplies. The death-loss among wildlife itself is discouraging. **This qualifies as a disaster as surely as a major flood or drought.** Extra feed will be made available. The National Guard is helping to clear roads. Normal snowplows don't touch this stuff. Dozers and rotary plows are required. The ranchers away from main roads have to wait and wait for their township roads to be cleared out. There isn't enough manpower or equipment on hand to deal with the number of roads and fields plugged up.

There are plenty of worries about the coming spring - wet fields, a rushed planting season, finding out about the death loss, cash flow problems, nutritionally deficient and weak calves, more death loss, fertility problems, low cattle prices, etc. Expensive bulls with frozen testicles are like a death loss. But, it's not the long term producers think about, at least right now. It is how to get through the day and to do what needs to be done.

**The upside** is they will have wonderful pastures, good subsoil moisture, dams full of water, a great first cutting of a hay crop and a cattle market on it's way up from rock bottom. Neighbors help neighbors. Families pull together. People get together to socialize, laugh and tell stories about the worst winter they hope ever to see.

# Stress On The Farm

The news is not good this March of 1997. Pork and meat prices have gone to the basement. There are record numbers of cattle and hogs yet to work their way through the system. The feed grain costs are high.

The highly industrialized poultry industry is extremely efficient, competitive and continues to grow. Large scale hog confinement systems are starting to be major players in the market and put great pressure on the small independent producer. For meat producers, the prospects for the next two years look dim.

For grain farmers, crop prices are good - although two years of poor weather has produced low and spotty yields. Without anything to sell, the high prices don't mean much.

Longtime, experienced farmers and livestock producers can weather the problems. They'll be around when the business climate improves. Low prices and debt problems spell serious cash flow problems for some producers. Many are faced with the possibility of going out of business.

Stress and worry are hitting a lot of folks. I've seen it in my office. I've heard it over the phone. Others tell me of their concern. It is not good.

There is anger about the price of meat in the stores. It hasn't dropped with the producer's lower earnings. Farmers could accept their plight easier if they could see the low prices being passed on to the consumer. Because there is tremendous concentration in the meat packing industry - three or four main corporations dominate the industry - there is suspicion of collusion.

Farmers work hard, put in long hours and take huge risks in an industry where their hard work is occasionally negated by market forces. Input costs continue to rise and advances in technology add pressures of their own.

**Farmers and emotions.** Farmers are socialized to a rural way of life, on the farm and in small communities. It is a neighborly world with lots of caring and personal interaction. They like being their own bosses They enjoy a kinship with nature and the outdoors. They are excellent problem-solvers and producers.

Farmers love what they do and are good at it. Many have inherited their land from their parents and have a strong goal of keeping the land in the family. It is a family dream and heritage for which farmers feel a keen sense of responsibility. They are loathe to leave everything they know and love.

Can you imagine the emotions, the hard work and the commitment to make it work, though times turn bad? The good years even out the bad - if they can make it through the bad. Hope is there. It is not a profession or a lifestyle one leaves easily.

Reality hits with a jolt. The lender has his or her own set of guidelines and assets to protect. Without an operating loan, farmers are out of business. Even if a loan is secured, the farmer has the anxiety of making it work or facing even bigger problems next year. Weather and prices - two big uncontrollable factors - will determine how things will go.

**Stress on the farm.** When things go wrong, farmers put in long hours, toss and turn at night and are racked with worry they can't shut down. They fight depression. They blame themselves. They feel anger and lash out at those around them - their families. Blaming large corporate farms that pose a threat to the economies of smaller farming operations is easy.

Working harder isn't the answer though it is the answer they know best. Putting in even longer hours adds to the stress level and can be counterproductive.

Farm women feel the stress of cutting back, making ends meet, working an off-farm job, and getting exhausted themselves. They worry about their husband and children. They especially worry about the quality of their marriage if their husband is withdrawing or blaming her for the difficulties. This is even a greater worry than the financial stress they are facing.

A farm crisis puts a marriage to the test and exposes some

underlying weaknesses in communication and problem-solving. Marital arguments and clashes are common. It is easy to blame others and to get irritated when things don't go right.

Most farmers are self reliant and take responsibility for solving their own problems. During times of high stress this virtue becomes a weakness. The best coping strategies involve turning to others for help - getting good information about options and alternatives and taking action. Farmers don't farm themselves out of trouble. They manage themselves out of trouble.

Supportive feedback from a spouse and other's that care can sustain people and help them see the bigger picture. There is something healing and helpful about getting problems talked out. By talking and sharing feelings, they put the problem outside the self and it becomes less threatening. The person is not the problem. The problem is the problem.

There is something comforting in knowing you are not alone and in talking with others who are in the same boat. It also helps to know what you are going through is normal even though it is painful.

# How Rural Couples React To Economic Pressures

During times of financial stress, how much difference does a spouse's emotional support make? Does it reduce depression? How does it affect self-confidence and feelings of control? Does emotional support differ in its effects on husbands and wives? Do farmers and non-farmers react differently to economic pressures?

These are a few of the questions addressed by a study involving the Iowa Youth and Family Services Project at Iowa State University.

Rural sociologist Frederick Lorenz and his colleagues reported a study of 388 rural families from eight central Iowa counties. These were two-parent families with one seventh grade child and one other sibling within four years of his or her age.

Of the families initially involved in the study, 34 percent were identified as living on farms though many were not farming. Twenty-two percent of the men reported their occupations as farmers. Twenty-two percent of the women were identified as homemakers.

The median age for husbands and wives was 39 and 37 respectively. The median education for both was 13 years.

In 1988, the survey measured economic pressures in terms of average per capita income and debt-to-asset ratios.

In 1989, the survey measured the actual economic adjustments families made, whether they were making ends meet, and if they felt satisfied with their economic situation.

At the same time, another measure was taken showing the amount of emotional support husbands and wives received from each other. In addition, each, person responded to items that indicated their sense of control or mastery over events taking place in their lives.

Finally, in 1990, symptoms of depression and emotional distress were measured. Here are some of their findings:

▶ Economic pressures affected feelings of control that in turn affected symptoms of depression. For both men and women, feelings of depression, anxiety and emotional distress are directly affected by their feelings of the lack of power or control they have over their lives.

Feelings of mastery are strongly enhanced by a spouse's emotional support. Emotional support supplies the confidence and self-assurance to cope actively with problems.

▶ For wives, low support from husbands during times of economic pressure was strongly related to their feelings of lack of control. However, research showed that farm women had significantly less depression if they felt loved and supported by their husbands.

The threat to her self-esteem may come more from feeling unloved and the deteriorating quality of her marriage than by poor economic conditions.

A husband's love and support for his wife during hard times will greatly affect her feelings of well-being. If a man is too depressed to be supportive, then a woman has to fall back on her own sense of control and strength to ward off depression.

▶ For rural men, the relationship between a supportive wife and a sense of control and self-confidence is important under low stress, stable economic conditions. During high stress conditions, a man's failure to cope with economic pressure represents a direct challenge to his self-worth despite the love and caring he receives from his wife.

Husbands with loving wives may feel like double failures. The wife is doing her part, but he feels he is failing as a provider. Rural men who complain about the lack of support from their "fair weather" wives may feel less supported because of their depression and  inaccurate perceptions of the support their wife actually is giving.

The key to alleviating their depression is getting back their sense of control and self-confidence.

# When Debt Comes In The Door, Love Goes Out The Window

When debt comes in the door, love goes out the window. What happens to a farm couple when persistent financial problems plague their farm operation?

Full-time farmers generally grow up on a farm, gain farm skills and knowledge, inherit land and get their start in farming through family support. This process completes a parental dream of keeping the farm in the family and having one or more families from the next generation maintain a foothold in agriculture.

The larger and more prosperous the farm, the more likely it is that the family attaches high value to family continuity on the farm. This is especially true where the farm family derives its income from the farm and has not had to rely on off-farm income for their living.

A sizable percentage of sons in these operations marry women with farm backgrounds themselves. Their lives as farmers are enclosed within the world of agriculture. They have absorbed the skills and values of a farm-based lifestyle.

How do they think when confronted by a situation where their farm income falls substantially? Full-time farmers are far more likely to seek a solution to their income problems within agriculture. They are more likely to work harder on the farm, tighten their belts and accept a lower standard of living. They are reluctant to shore up their income through non-farm work.

This strong commitment to farming is underscored by the expectation that they will "arm their way out of trouble." If anything, they are likely to increase their energies and investment in farming to make it work.

Their lifestyle, their close social ties to friends and relatives, their familiarity with the land and the community, their knowledge base and farming skills, their commitment to keeping land in the family, even their very identity - these things are centered in farming. It is a different world from other occupations.

Full-time farmers with this background lack interest in pursuing alternative careers. They lack enthusiasm for taking off-farm employment. They definitely aren't interested in giving up farming. During a financial crisis, they continue to look at means of increasing their production and their investment in the farm business. They modernize their methods wherever possible.

What does that mean for the farm family? What is functional for the farmer's goals and maintaining the farm business may be unsatisfactory to other members of his family.

Under these circumstances, family members can be exploited, tied to the farm, and pushed into even longer days and harder work. This happens within an emotional climate of depression, anxiety, high stress and unreasonable demands. Working harder on the farm and adjusting to a lower standard of living for the sake of continuing in full-time farming may not seem like an acceptable alternative to the rest of the family.

A wife withdraws her support to what she sees as a debilitating and losing enterprise. Without his wife's support, the husband feels less in control and even more subject to economic pressures. Under these conditions, he is more prone to depression. He is wrapped up in his problems and doesn't offer much support to his wife. His lack of support coupled with economic problems increases the feelings of loss of control in her life and the likelihood of her becoming depressed.

Her efforts to suggest alternatives such as leaving the farm are rebuffed as out-of-hand. Her efforts to provide honest feedback and correct mistakes being made aren't heeded. She doesn't feel like he really wants her true feelings anyway. The farm and farming; his feelings and his needs, are definitely and emphatically put first. This is a rude awakening. Her happiness and the happiness of the children aren't being considered.

To her, keeping the farm in the family, having her husband always be a farmer, are negotiable compared to the well-being of everyone involved. She is surprised by his lack of flexibility and stubborn clinging to dreams that are sinking the family. She begins to lose respect for his decisions.

He makes things worse by criticizing her lack of commitment. He is mired in worries and anxieties. The farm is all he wants to talk about. He is depressed and depressing.

Occasionally he explodes in anger. He accuses her of withdrawing her support just when he needs her the most.

It is true. She is scared by her reaction. She doesn't care how he feels. The feelings that are supposed to be there aren't there.

Now what? He's not an ogre, an alcoholic, a wife-beater or a skirt chaser. He is an honest, hard-working farmer. His very being is tied to the land regardless of what the emotional price might be to him and his family. The farm crisis brings out how differently they each really feel about the things they want in life. They are pulling in different directions.

Who would understand that something like a farm could drive them apart? There doesn't seem to be many other explanations for their troubles. Their differences about the worth of farming became apparent when debt came in the door.

# Film Shows Struggle Of Farm Families

Public television presented a documentary called, "The Farmer's Wife." The program documents the struggle of a Nebraska farm family between 1995 and 1997 in their heroic struggle to save their farm. The program educates the general public on the stresses of modern day farming.

The raw drama of their lives is captured in their daily journey to cope with powerful forces. Farm women will identify with Juanita Buschkoetter's dedication to her husband Darrel and her three daughters. This is a must see for a farm family in similar circumstances.

Here are some of the dilemmas captured by the film-maker David Sutherland.

- The toll of off-farm work on both Juanita and Darrel as they alternately take off-farm employment to keep their farm afloat.

- Darrel feeling obligated to do work for his father who can't quite approve of his son's talents. The film shows the delicate relationship of a father and son who can't quite be close despite a lifetime of farming together. The relationship between the father-in-law and daughter-in-law is strained.

The film shows the process of transferring the farm from one generation to the next. Darrel's father has his own adjustments to make. He grudgingly learns to respect his son and daughter-in-law, though he can't bring himself to express it.

- Juanita is forced to take a cleaning job, get food stamps for the family and eventually goes back to college to get an A.A. degree. She gets a better job that provides more income for the family. Her guilt in leaving her daughters is palpable.

The film shows her mental and physical exhaustion in dealing with and in caring for her three daughters and her struggling husband. Juanita also deals with the pressures of the farm finances, off-farm work, and keeping up with her college classes. She pitches bales and vaccinates hogs. Darrel wants her full-time on the farm but their circumstances won't allow it. She is the heroic figure - the glue that keeps everything together in spite of incessant worry and stress.

- Juanita isn't supported by her family who feels that farming is a mistake and encourages her to leave the farm and her husband if necessary. Their attitude isolates her from family support. Juanita's mother didn't like the marriage from the start and won't listen to Juanita's problems.

- The cars are old, the equipment breaks down, and their clothing is second-hand. They have to scrape by.

- They have tension with their lender and have to face their creditors as they work out their debts. They face pain and humiliation.

- Darrel is insecure and lacks confidence. The hard drought years have made him bitter and angry. He scapegoats his anger on to Juanita and others. He is jealous and insecure about her mixing with others at work and school and is afraid she will reject him and their farming lifestyle.

She takes a stand and Darrel chooses counseling to preserve their marriage. Juanita is flexible enough to leave farming but is patient with Darrel's dream. She leads his fight to keep the farm. Juanita takes over the farm finances and makes the hard decisions that keeps the family and the farm together. He appreciates her strength and love. In the end he matures and becomes strong enough either to leave or to be much happier in farming.

- The endless work day of the farm family is portrayed in its grinding detail. The conflict between Darrel and Juanita over Darrel's role with the children and the home is graphically shown. Again Darrel gradually becomes a more helpful and supportive father once he is beyond the crushing stress of debt. His future in farming is more secure.

- You can feel the joy and satisfaction of a good harvest and an upturn in their fortune. They experience the small joys of family life on a farm. You can sense the wholesomeness of it all when it works well.

- You learn of their dependence on weather and how life hangs in the balance, both in terms of economics and the tasks that have to be done.

- I admired Darrel's general know-how in fixing things. That ability to trouble shoot problems is probably the quintessential skill in farming.

This documentary is painful yet full of hope. Their triumph is heart-warming. This will be a difficult viewing experience for farm families who are in similar precarious positions. I hope that viewers can visualize a different ending - an ending where a family in a similar situation makes a successful transition out of agriculture. That story needs to be told also.

# All This Milking Is Killing Me

Dear Dr. Farmer,

My name is Don. I'm a dairy farmer. I'm 46 years old and I've been farming all my life. My two kids are gone and are leading their own lives. I milk 80 cows and run 450 acres of land, some of which I own and some I rent. My wife is an RN at a local hospital. She helps me when she can.

It's hard to find good help nowadays. It seems like kids don't want to work. I would like to phase out of farming just a little but still stay in it somewhat.

I'm up at 4:00 a.m. every morning. I love planting crops - hay, corn and beans. I don't mind putting in 12 to 14 hours a day but to go in that barn at 5:00a.m. and milk cows yet - that is killing me! I would like to sell the cows and still farm the land, but when the cows go, so does the income!

At my age, I don't want to work for someone else after being my own boss all these years. My barn burned down several years ago and I built a new one plus a new heifer facility later. If I sell my farm it will take care of the debt load and capital gains tax but not leave me enough money to build a house.

To put it bluntly, it is hard to get out of farming. With milk prices the way they are, you have to milk more cows and I don't want to. I just want to slow down a little! If you have any suggestions, let me know! - Don

Dear Don,

Thanks for sharing your worries with me. Right now your emotions are in control. You are being worn down by dairying and you don't see any way out. Take the emotion out of it by doing a detailed financial analysis of your farm. Chances are you will have some assets to work with.

What do you want to do with your life? It's not too late if you have a clear idea of what you want. If you don't know what you want, a career counselor could be a sounding board for you as you sort through what you really want to do.

Leaving the farm or changing your farming operation doesn't make you a failure. It is making a change to meet your goals. It is a willingness to use your resources to further your goals. If you develop that kind of thinking a whole world of choices opens up to you.

Look at your farm as an asset. I don't know what the market is for a dairy farm in your area. If you can sell it go down the road and buy another farm that is more suitable to the type of farming you want to do.

You could look at converting your existing farm to another type of farm. How about planting a specialty crop that grows in your area or converting to a beef cow operation? Depending on how you are set up, you could lease out the dairy and continue to do crops.

You have more options than you realize. Find a farm financial consultant who can come in and help you analyze your possibilities. Right now things seem overwhelming. Play "what if" games and cost out various options. Decisions don't seem so bad if they are broken down into small steps.

Be adaptable. Take a chance. Doing something you hate is no way to go in life. It will take a little creative imagination, some courage and some good advice but you can make changes despite your circumstances.

Sincerely, Dr. Val Farmer

# Reactions To Letter From Trapped Dairyman

I received some letters from people describing plights similar to the one described by the dairyman who felt trapped by his investment. Others were familiar with his situation and offered advice on how to deal with it.

**A Wisconsin woman wrote** that after she and her husband raised a large family none of the children were interested in taking over the farm. "They all have good jobs and have the weekend free. They are willing to help out when we need it, but don't want to be tied down seven days a week."

She and her husband have contemplated selling the cows, but the proceeds from the sale coupled with the milk income for the year would create a huge tax liability. She feels trapped.

Recently a cow knocked her down in the barn and she broke her hip. She was unable to help milk or do any farm work for three to six months. When she went to file for temporary social security disability, she found out that, despite filing joint income tax returns all their married lives, all of the farm income was in her husband's name and social security number. She was not entitled to benefits.

"I can appeal the Social Security decision and draw on my husband's number, but then he would receive less. And I won't do that. Basically I have worked on the farm for forty years for nothing . . . When I get to be 62, I can only draw 37% of what my husband gets from Social Security - which won't be very much.

"I just want other farm wives to know that they have to have a separate income to get Social Security. Just have your husband pay you a wage. It can still go into the same account, but you will at least get credit for the work you do in the eye of the government."I am going to try and work to change the law on that."

**Another small town business owner from Minnesota** wrote that she has tried to sell her business that performs a vital community service. But because of a stagnant and shrinking small town economy a young family would have trouble making a living from it. Her husband had to find other employment. They tried to sell the business but there were no takers. She realized that this isn't what she wanted to do with the rest of her life.

"My husband says to "lock the door" but I can't do that to the town or to the memory of the previous generations of family members in the business. I can't be the one to lock the door, therefore I'm also as trapped as the farmer milking cows every morning at 5:00 a.m." She wondered if I had any insights into her situation.

The emotion of keeping a business (for farmers, it's the land) in the family has a powerful effect on business decisions. It is a big hurdle to cross but once you let go more alternatives open up and better economic decisions are made. In one situation, three businesses from adjoining small communities combined their resources under a single management and formed a more viable business.

There were a few letters with helpful advice for the worn out dairyman.

**A vibrant and active 82-year-old farm woman from Michigan wrote,** "I've been down that road. I moved through freshening heifers to deacons to feeders to cow-calf - also boarding cattle and calves. I backed into the sheep business. They were supposed to eat grass around the farmstead to reduce the fire hazard. Now I wouldn't trade them for the world."

This dairywoman turned sheep farmer then went into detail about her management of the lambs and timing on markets. She enclosed financial information comparing cows and calves with ewes and lambs.

She enclosed an article of a Michigan farm publication that described a family being forced out of the dairy business. She comments, " With the current theory of 'get big or get out' and with numerous small herds going out, it would seem like some kind of lease arrangement should be possible to keep from 'killing' the guy. Another thought: how about a dairy student from the state ag school who has the desire but not the money to milk? Give him or her a stake in the future -not just straight wages."

**A South Dakota farmer** gave the following brief advice. "Advertise the milk cows and have an auction or take them to an auction. Your cows will sell well. Buy back some beef cows and you will have money left over to pay down your debt. Enjoy life! It's the only one you get. Good luck."

**A farmer from Indiana** wrote, "Be advised that paying capital gains taxes is unnecessary! Transfer property to a Charitable Remainder Trust before selling. That will eliminate capital gains. The owner still receives all proceeds."

# The Most Vulnerable Farmers

Which farmers have the most difficulty coping with the threat of losing a family farm? Here are five points to consider why farmers are vulnerable to suicide and depression.

1. **The all-encompassing dream.** Farmers who have lived their lives "living, eating and breathing" farming will not feel like they have alternatives or options for other kinds of satisfying work: "Look at me, a 40-year-old man. I can hardly spell my name. I know nothing but work. How am I supposed to earn a living? The only thing I can think of is breaking my back for some other farmer."

Farmers who have had little or no experience living away from the farm or their rural communities are especially vulnerable. Farming has been their "whole" life, all they know. Their self-esteem and hopes are tied up in succeeding in that which they love. They have little conception or experience with other things they might love or enjoy. The older the farmer is, the more devoted he has been to his dream, the more vulnerable he becomes.

The tenacity and denial with which a farmer holds on and fights for his farm increases with his lack of preparedness or willingness to do other things. He is fighting for his life, his prized view of himself. For him, there is no other choice. When the actual loss comes, it will hit like a ton of bricks.

2. **High expectations.** The vulnerable man takes himself and life seriously. He expects a lot out of himself. He strives. He achieves. He pours himself into his work. His approach to solving problems is action-oriented. His work shows pride and tradition.

He is not used to failure. He is hard on himself for not being in control. He is prone to guilt when something goes wrong. In losing his farm, his self-esteem is threatened. He fights back by working harder. His pride and his heart will keep him there when his head tells him to go.

3. **Dependency on others.** The vulnerable man not only expects a great deal of himself but from others as well. He lives in a world where people do what they ought to do. He lives in a "nice" world where people are kind, just and fair. He takes care of others and he expects others to take care of him.

This dependency and trust may be placed in his wife, family, parents, lender, business associates, neighbors or in the government. He expects them to live up to their word. He does his part; they do their part. He wants and expects a great deal from others but he can't admit it. He is sensitive and angry when they let him down.

His dependency on others is hidden from himself by a myth of independence. In a time of crisis, he comes face to face with feelings of abandonment, injustice, rage and anxiety. This suddenly revealed dependence elicits a hostile reaction towards those people or institutions on whom he depends or has depended.

He will also experience panic regarding his new feelings of being powerless and defective in his fight to keep his dream. His kind and nice universe, of which he was at the center, is crumbling. This is a terribly disillusioning and frightening experience.

4. **Overcontrol or undercontrol of aggressive fantasy.** To counteract the feelings of self-devaluation, the farmer in crisis will have many aggressive images and fantasies go through his mind. These fantasies may involve striking out or back at the source of the threat or at oneself. These are normal feelings and images for the circumstances.

Vulnerable men get into trouble two ways. The first is that they get scared of their thoughts and emotions racing out of control. They judge themselves harshly by their high "nice guy" moral standards and become fearful of doing something wrong.

For men who have lived their lives keeping a tight reign on their emotions and aggressive feelings, this is scary. They may also feel it is sinful. They fear losing control.

The second way farmers get into trouble is that some may be captivated by their aggressive imagery and consciously entertain thoughts of revenge. These thoughts preserve their sense of power and control even though objectively they may be helpless to change the course of events. They walk a fine line of having their violent feelings spill over into aggression against themselves and others. And they know it. This is also scary.

5. **Emotional isolation and withdrawal.** Vulnerable men are not used to turning to others for emotional support. They choose to "go it alone" and keep their own counsel. They have had little experience with solving problems through reflective listening. Actions are what count.

When they are confused and don't know what to do, they retreat and hide their feelings of self-doubt, humiliation and inadequacy from themselves and others. They do not see others as a resource and reject help when it is offered.

What kind of farmers are most vulnerable to a catastrophic loss? It is farmers who live for a dream, expect a lot out of themselves, have high moral standards and have contained intense emotions over a lifetime in order to get along. They have trusted and expected the best from others and value self-reliance for themselves.

It is ironic that the ingredients for living a successful life make them the most vulnerable. During times of crisis, these qualities can take the form of rigidity, stubbornness, guilt, blaming and social withdrawal - the ingredients for failure to adapt.

# Why People Attempt Suicide

Dr. Roy Baumeister, psychologist at Case Western Reserve University in Cleveland, Ohio has outlined a theory of suicidal death. The following questions and answers are based on his research and ideas.

**Why do people attempt or commit suicide?** A desire to escape from painful thoughts, emotions and self-awareness motivates the vast majority of suicides from psychological causes. Personal or family honor motivates other types of suicide, but these are rare in our culture.

**How does a person get to a suicidal state of mind?** Baumeister outlines six steps on the way to suicidal thinking.

**1. A current situation falls far below a person's expectations.** There are either unrealistic high expectations or recent setbacks, specific failures and stresses - or a combination of both. If expectations are low, setbacks won't produce suicide. If events are unusually bad, risk of suicide increases. It is the scope of difference between expectations and events that causes the problem. Societies that emphasize individual pride, shame, and self-awareness have higher rates of suicide.

**2. Personal blame is assumed for disappointments.** This is especially true when the self-blaming person believes their undesirable shortcomings are permanent and are likely to cause future difficulties. A person may compare their behavior unfavorably with past levels of higher performance or believes he or she cannot live up to what other people expect.

**3. A painful state of mind is created when people judge themselves as inadequate, incompetent, unattractive or guilty.** Feelings of low self-esteem and powerlessness are common. Suicidal people see others in a favorable light in contrast to their own harsh assessment of themselves.

**4. Bad feelings result when they unfavorably compare themselves against their own standards.** The most common emotions are depression and anxiety, though anger may also be present. They fail to redefine a setback in a more positive light or make the changes necessary to meet a new reality.

**5. In an attempt to escape from bad feelings, people try to stop meaningful thought.** An individual hopes to feel better by either ceasing to feel emotion, ceasing to blame oneself for recent events or ceasing to be aware of self. By refusing meaningful thought, they stop all three. This results in emotional emptiness and numbness, something like boredom. When negative emotions and thoughts break through, increasingly stronger means are tried to stop or block them. Suicide edges closer and closer as a solution for unbearable feelings.

**6. Avoiding meaningful thought lowers inhibitions which makes suicide attempts easier.** Avoiding thoughts about social and religious norms, obligations to others and desires for the future removes internal barriers to particular actions. Actions no longer have the meaning they once did.

**What does a person do to stop meaningful thought?** They become passive about long term goals and important decisions. They stop striving and avoid decisions, responsibilities and planning. Their behavior becomes more aimless, mindless or impulsive. They show a lack of emotion - especially positive emotion. They are either bored or vaguely unhappy.

- Focus is on the present, on immediate tasks and details and on concrete situations.
- Taking meaningful, constructive action is resisted. They stop trying new things and are unwilling to explore alternatives.
- Reasoning becomes rigid. They avoid new thoughts, ideas or interpretations.
- Wishful thought, irrational thought or fantasy is preferred. Fantasy allows the mind to escape the immediate present and is an alternative to dealing with the real meanings in one's life.

When people achieve a low level of thinking and emotions,

they are less rational and have reduced inhibitions. Death in the short run seems preferable to emotional suffering and the painful awareness of being inadequate. Long range implications of death are not considered because of the short term focus.

Preoccupation with suicide or a suicidal plan gets the person involved with "here and now" details and techniques while eliminating the need to think about the future. The past doesn't matter either because it has nearly ended and will no longer cause grief, worry or anxiety.

**What are the more positive ways of reacting to trauma?** A long term response to trauma involves searching for higher meaning to explain changed situations. Religion and/or belief in oneself helps to show the way to find new meaning and consolation in misfortune. Instead of retreating from thought and bad feelings, a traumatized person can actively try to understand the new circumstance and place it into a larger, more hopeful context.

**How can a suicidal person be helped?** Intervention can be directed at breaking any link in the chain that leads from disappointment and failure to a suicidal attempt. A traumatized person can be helped by learning to have realistic expectations, take blame off themselves and build self-esteem, search for higher meaning about setbacks, see the future in a more positive light, reacquaint themselves with their normal fears and beliefs about death, accept family responsibilities and other duties, strengthen family ties and social bonds, be more effective in managing negative feelings and take a more meaningful perspective on their own actions.

Suicidal people need to think, talk and face themselves and the problem rather than retreating into a self-defeating attempt to shut down their minds and emotions.

*CHAPTER THREE*

# HOPE TO COPE WITH HARD TIMES

## Dr. Farmer's
## Best Advice On The Farm Crisis

North American farmers are facing an unprecedented siege of low prices. The economics of farming are poor. It takes a lot of money to farm - whether it be land payments, repayment of operating loans, the high costs of inputs, and high cost of living. Income from crops doesn't begin to stretch far enough.

This isn't an ordinary profession or business that one can walk away from at a moment's notice. The debts, assets, tax liabilities, and contractual obligations can be overwhelming. The ideal way to leave farming is through an orderly process that takes place over a two to three year time frame. That is just from the economic standpoint.

From the emotional standpoint, farmers have to give up a profession and lifestyle in which they have spent a lifetime learning. They have to reconcile themselves to leaving land that has been in the family for generations. They have to overcome their fears of finding something else to do in life that is as rewarding as farming. They have to face leaving a community of family and friends and starting over in an unknown world that won't care in the same way.

To leave farming, farmers have to turn their backs on their traditional formula for success: commitment, persistence, hard work and faith – faith in themselves, faith in God, faith in a profession where the business cycle eventually turns good.

Here is my best advice for farmers trying to cope with decisions of this magnitude:

***1. Decision-making.*** Be familiar with your own financial numbers, equity, liabilities, cost of production, cash flow, and outlook for future prices. Face this reality with input from your lender and other financial advisers. Don't hide from the facts. Acknowledge them to whoever needs to know. Don't let your pride get in the way of making hard decisions.

Find your hope - your best scenario for survival – and subject it to a rigorous critique to see if it passes muster. If it does, work to make it happen.

**Aggressively gather information.** Just as love takes away fear, so does knowledge. Find out about resources. Find out what you need to know. This year is a new situation, a harsh reality that has to be faced and recognized for what it is. If your existing equity permits the choice, then it is a judgment call whether to fight one's way through a tough situation or to admit that farming isn't profitable and not worth the emotional and financial risks. Find out about what others know and have done who have been in your shoes.

**Decide on what is best for the family.** This is the standard by which you should judge your decisions. A farm is a means to an end - the happiness and well being of the family. If keeping a farm becomes an end in itself, then the farm is a liability that interferes with rational decision–making. Past generations would applaud your efforts to look after your family in the best way possible. That is what they did by uprooting themselves and searching out a life in a distant land.

**Talk about your situation.** Talk through your inner emotions. Talk some more. Share your thoughts with your spouse and in other confidential relationships. Talking will help you become more objective about the problem. It will clarify your thinking. You will also gain the input and support of those with whom you share ideas.

Going through a crisis alone makes for poorer decisions and depression becomes more likely.

**Avoid guilt and self-recrimination.** This is not a personal failure. There is nothing to be ashamed of. Your dilemma isn't a result of poor management. It is a reflection on the world farm economy, farm technology, business trends, and a host of weather and ag policy decisions that extend far beyond the fence line.

**2. Personal coping.** As an individual, you can do the following things to manage your stress and stop it from spoiling your life and spilling over onto the lives of your loved ones.

A positive attitude is crucial. You can't control some of the events that happen to you but you can control how you react to them. Acceptance of losses, setbacks and disappointments helps us deal with life's problems and injustices. Worry about the things you can do something about.

**Renew your faith.** There is purpose to life. It is a test and a challenge. Decide what these things mean. Seek and find spiritual comfort for dealing with adversity and suffering. From bad can come good. Find the silver lining – the personal and spiritual growth that comes from hard times.

If you look for the silver lining, the cloud doesn't look as dark. Someday when you tell the story of your life, some of your most defining moments, moments that changed you into a better human being, will have happened during times of trial and struggle. Be patient with life. The turning points in life come from humbling experiences where the only place to go is to your knees.

Take pleasure in the new things you've learned about life, love, friendships, family, your spouse, and yourself. Take pleasure in your talents, health, spiritual understanding, the beauty and mystery of nature, and opportunities to brighten the lives of others.

**Use your sense of humor.** A sense of humor can give you room for your spirit to breathe. Leisure, hobbies and wholesome diversions take your mind off the distant future and will bring you pleasure when you need it the most.

During stressful times it is distractions, humor, family fun, light-hearted moments, and showing love that puts you and your family above the crisis instead of below it. Laugh at the absurdity, irony and unfairness of life.

*3. Family coping.* Here are some things you can do in your marriage and in your family to help one another:

Cooperate with the workload. Manage the stress that comes with off-farm employment and auxiliary enterprises. If one or both of you are working off the farm, the stress, fatigue and irritability factor will likely strain your relationship. Make sure you are cooperative and supportive of each other's workloads and responsibilities. Even if you have nothing else to offer, you can offer deep understanding and support.

**Go through it together.** Open up and share your inner thoughts and feelings. We all need a confidential outlet for the things of our heart. A crisis is an opportunity to share deeply with those who we care about.

Marital relationships are based on respect, trust and mutual influence. You need to share the big picture. You need to share the details of your lives. You need to talk through difficult problems and know you can solve them. Your basic goals and values unite you, even if your opinions differ.

**Watch your spending,** both business and family living expenses. Be flexible. Make whatever changes need to be made. Make the tough decisions together.

**Listen to your spouse and children.** Let them know what you are going through. Listen to them. You aren't the only person facing a challenge. Find out how they perceive the situation. Your spouse and your children all need to share their concerns with you as well and to be greeted with an understanding heart.

Enlist their cooperation. They can be a bright spot in your life when stress is high. By supporting one another through a difficult time, you can strengthen the bonds that really matter with those you love.

**Communicate with partners in family business.** Be open and honest with them. Find out what they are thinking and feeling. Many heads are better than one. If you get support from family, it doesn't matter what the world thinks.

Show an increase of love. Go out of your way to be kind and loving to each other. Soothe one another. Ease each other's burden. Be the first to give love. Be kind to those you love.

**Avoid unnecessary conflict.** Watch your temper. Don't blame. Don't withdraw. Don't pick a fight or escalate a fight. If your spouse is angry, listen and only listen. Don't give advice, criticism or respond in anger. Listening is the best thing you can do. Your turn will come.

**Family fun.** If there is ever a time when you need to let your hair down and make some fun, this is it. Make memories. Lighten up. A farm is a wonderful place to have light-hearted moments.

These are the things you have control over. If worst comes to worst, it won't seem so bad if you have developed a better perspective on life and have grown closer together in your family. It can be a good year. The rest will take care of itself.

Family farming is special but not so special that it becomes more important than marriage, family, health, mental health, and faith in God. If you should choose to quit farming, remember this: you and your family can be happy somewhere else, doing something else.

This is life. Life is change. Life has possibilities. God has another plan for you. Your brain, your heart and your faith have to work together. Know that your life and those you love are far more precious than cruel economics and unwanted change.

# Why Some Farmers Cope Better Than Others

This analysis of differences on coping abilities in crisis situations was described by behavioral health specialist Jeanne Schaefer and psychologist Rudolf Moos of Stanford Medical Center.

What do you do when the rug is jerked out from under you? Do some people land on their feet while others stay on the floor contemplating their misery? What makes the difference in how farm families react to misfortune?

Some events would overwhelm anybody. People vary in their coping abilities based on their differing past histories and personal qualities. A lot depends on mental attitude. Social support is an important factor. Let's go ahead and follow the rug jerking analogy in its various ramifications.

*1. Events:* **Severity and duration.** If you break your back in a fall, you are going to feel worse than if you sprain an ankle. It is not so bad if you are disabled for a few days instead of several months.

**Amount of deprivation.** The injury causes you to lose your occupation, your home and forces you to move to another place. That feels worse than missing four innings in a softball game because of the sprain.

**Blocked goals.** The injury means you have to give up your dream of being a professional football player and you flounder around trying to figure out what else to do.

**Suddenness.** Instead of a rug being jerked from under you, supposing your mother-in-law notifies you she wants the rug back she loaned you. You have a month to figure out how to replace it.

**Misery loves company.** It feels better when there were eight people on the rug and you all took a tumble versus being alone on that rug.

*2. Personal qualities:* **Religion and philosophical commitment.** Falling flat on the floor isn't so bad when you figure out that

God didn't pull the rug, or if he did, He did it for a good reason. You figure that life isn't fair, that people are meant to grow and respond to challenges and things will be OK.

**Self-confidence.** You've had other rugs jerked in the past and you've always figured out how to manage. (Maybe the fall wasn't as bad in the past. You have a confident feeling you will be able to get off the deck and get going again.)

**Help-seeking.** Since you've been down here before, you've learned how important it is to call for help right away and let other people take over rather than trying to get up on your own and take another tumble.

*3. Social Support:* **Soothed and comforted.** Within a day of the fall, you had many visitors, phone calls and cards. Your wife was at your side in the hospital stroking your head and reassuring you that things would work out. Your best friend dropped everything and came by. An associate who had a similiar fall lived by himself, had few friends and his parents lived four states away. He didn't do as well. He experienced more stress and more problems even when he was back on this feet.

**Sounding board.** You had a chance to talk through your grief, your worries, your fears. It feels good to have someone listen to you.

**Practical support.** You ask questions and exchange ideas on how to get by. Your friend gives you important advice on where to go for rehabilitation and what he did when he had a rug pulled out from under him. He doesn't minimize the problems and helps you become aware of issues you'll need to deal with.

**Loving family.** Your family shows you love and concern. They are there for you. You and your wife have had a happy marriage and you have supported her when she took a fall of her own. Another friend and his wife were having serious marriage problems. When he had a rug jerked from under him, she wasn't very sympathetic.

**New sources of support.** You join a self-help group for victims of rug jerkers. They are quite helpful and give good advice.

They know some of the struggles you are facing and the best way to deal with them.

**4. _Appraisal and problem-solving:_ Seek information.** You are hungry to know everything about rug falls and coping with being on the floor. You read and ask questions in order to understand what has happened. You get ideas on what to do. This gives you a sense of control, competence and mastery over the new situation. Being on the floor isn't quite so scary.

**Redefining the problem.** You figure out that being on the floor isn't such a bad place to be. You see things from floor level that helps you decide to do things differently when you get on your feet again. You decide to be more loving to your family because you can never tell when a rug might be jerked.

**Blame.** If you could have foreseen the rug being jerked, you take responsibility and learn from it. You see it as a one time event with a specific cause and not because of a deep-seated character flaw of being prone to pratfalls. You don't lie there stuck on the floor brooding and angrily thinking you don't deserve to be down there in the first place.

**Emotional control.** Your friend is lying there being angry, confused, scared, worried and depressed. He doesn't know what to do next. You have enough emotional control to think your way through the difficulty.

**Active problem-solving.** You face reality and start dealing with it. When the effects of the jerked rug can't be undone, you grieve, accept the reality and adjust to changes you have to make. Either way, a positive outlook will put the whole rug problem in a better perspective.

# How Thoughts and Emotions Are Connected

How do farmers adapt to devastating circumstances over which they have little control? Here is a description of the coping process for dealing with high stress.

**Positive Coping.** The most successful technique has to do with understanding and altering the source of the threat. This is problem-solving.

Farmers who make their living by problem-solving and reacting to changing circumstances now have to be flexible and adapt when the big picture goes haywire.

A second method of dealing with stress is to examine priorities and redefine goals because of new circumstances. People reaffirm their worth and the importance of their primary relationships despite the economic hardships.

Setbacks are redefined into a larger and more hopeful understanding about life. Religious faith plays a role in helping people endure losses and hardships.

Farmers who have been normally positive, flexible and moderate in their risk-taking, who are easy to get along with, determined, conscientious and hardworking will come out OK. It may take a little time.

It will not be pleasant. The days of worry, anxiety and fear will fade and the farmers' usual hope, confidence and enthusiasm will reappear.

**Negative Coping.** The most vulnerable farmers feel overwhelmed by their emotions. They attempt to regulate their emotions by denial, wishful thinking, self-blame, tension-reduction, self-isolation and by blaming others.

In their private ruminations and worry, they see themselves as the problem. In seeking solitude for their pain and confusion, they don't get the feedback they need about how normal they are. Their private effort to gain self-control interferes with a problem-solving style and keeps them from the useful ideas and caring that others have to offer.

Where do emotions come from? They come from the way people evaluate the implications of their circumstances and personal well-being. Thoughts about harm and benefits produce one's emotional state.

Each negative emotion is produced by a - particular type of appraised harm while positive emotions come from appraised benefits.

A study by psychologist Craig Smith, at Vanderbilt University, and his colleagues, found that each distant emotion is associated with its own distinct core theme.

**Emotion : Core theme**
Guilt : Self-blame
Anger : Other-blame
Fear, anxiety : Danger, threat
Sadness : Helplessness
Hope, challenge : Optimism
Happiness : Success

Positive copers judge their own history of being effective problem-solvers. This positive feeling about themselves contributes to their flexibility in finding a way to adapt to the crisis.

Positive copers communicate well and seek support from others. Talking through their situation helps them gain control over their emotions and refocus on an action-oriented, problem-solving style.

The more threatening the circumstances, the greater the need to turn to others for caring and support.

Negative copers have more intense negative emotions such as fear, hostility, guilt and sadness - which interfere with their appraisal of their ability to cope.

The problem is not the stressful event per se, but the way they think about their own coping skills that immobilizes their problem-solving orientation.

Negative emotions are the problem. Negative emotions come from persistent, well-established irrational thoughts built around certain core themes:

▶ An angry person needs to examine whether his or her assumptions about injustice and blame are valid and reasonable.

▶ A depressed person needs to understand his or her own power to change circumstances through solving problems. They need to define and work toward attainable goals.

▶ A person saddled with self-blame needs to reevaluate his or her inability to control everything. They need to put extenuating circumstances into perspective.

# When There Is A Will, There Is A Way

DIRECTIONS: Read each item carefully. Use this scale to select the number that best describes you: "1" means definitely false, "2" means mostly false, "3" means mostly true, "4" means definitely true.

--- 1. I can think of many ways to get out of a jam.
--- 2. I energetically pursue my goals.
--- 3. I feel tired most of the time.
--- 4. There are lots of ways around any problem.
--- 5. I am easily downed in an argument.
--- 6. I can think of many ways to get the things in life that are most important to me.
--- 7. I worry about my health.
--- 8. Even when others get discouraged, I know I can find a way to solve my problem.
--- 9. My experiences have prepared me well for my future.
--- 10. I've been pretty successful in life.
--- 11. I usually find myself worrying about something.
--- 12. I meet the goals I've set for myself.

This is the Hope Scale developed by psychologist C.R. Snyder of the University of Kansas. To get your score, add up the total from items 1, 2, 4, 6, 8, 9, 10 and 12. High hope is defined as 24 and above. Low hope is defined as 16 and below.

The other items are distractors. About 50 percent of people taking the Hope Scale have high hope, while about 10 percent have low hope.

To define hope, Snyder takes the expression, "When there is a will, there is a way," and divides it in two parts. The "will" is the willpower or energy to get moving toward one's goals. He calls this "agency." The "way" is the perceived ability to get there. He calls this aspect of hope "pathways."

To get your agency score, add items 2, 9, 10 and 12. To get your pathways score, add items 1, 4, 6 and 8. When people think about goals, they analyze both their mental energy and whether there are ways to attain their goals. People with willful determination continue to generate more pathways if their preferred pathway is blocked. Views of their past successes, failures and capabilities are crucial to the development of hope.

**Not always true.** The expression, "When there is a will, there is a way," is, not always true. Sometimes circumstances are such that we cannot get to our goal, no matter how strong our determination may be. That is reality. To maintain high hope, people need to sense both a strong sense of agency and available pathways.

People with high hope have many advantages. When compared to people with low hope, they have more goals, have more difficult goals, have success at achieving their goals, perceive their goals as challenges, have greater happiness and less distress, have superior coping skills, recover better from physical injury, and report less burnout.

**Hope is more than intelligence.** Snyder found that hope predicts these positive outcomes while intelligence does not. Intelligence gives a person a chance at their goals while hope generates the determination and the pathways to success. Hopeful people define their goals in concrete ways and break them down into step-by-step sub-goals. They keep their hope alive because they can sense progress. Snyder's studies show that people with high hope:

- use self-talk about succeeding;
- think of difficulties encountered as reflecting wrong strategy, not lack of talent;
- think of goals and setbacks as challenges, not failures;
- recall past successes
- take in stories of how other people have succeeded;
- cultivate friends with whom they can talk;
- find role models to emulate;
- exercise, eat and rest well; laugh at oneself, especially when stuck;
- set new goals when pathways to a current goal are absolutely blocked;
- reward themselves for small goal attainment on the way to larger, long-term goals;
- educate themselves for specific skills as well as learning how to learn.

**Effectiveness is the key.** In his theory of hope, Snyder believes that emotion is a by-product of how effective we are in the pursuit of our goals. To give people hope, he feels it is important to help them think through their goals, reevaluate their capacities and explore various pathways to success.

Parents, teachers, managers, coaches, partners, managers and counselors can help bring about change by working on the two components of hope. Snyder finds that people become energized when they clarify or define a goal. Once they have focus, the pathways become obvious. By reevaluating themselves and developing self-confidence, energy to work for goals kicks in. Problem-solving activities create enthusiasm about goals.

When there is a will, is there a way? I hope so.

# Explaining Hardships Helps
# Heal The Teller

*We are facing an economic shortfall. We couldn't plant this spring because our fields were waterlogged. This past winter, spring and early summer were very unusual - the rains never stopped. A typical farmer, I held out hope right to the end.*

*I started to blame myself because there were a few days in early spring when I could have tried something. I felt we would hit a decent dry spell sooner or later. I mortgaged some land to buy a piece of ground in case one of my boys wants to farm someday.*

*We weathered the '80s with some hardship but came out OK. I didn't dream that we could ever get overextended again but it happened. I took a job driving a truck. We tightened our family budget. We are trying to figure out how to make ends meet. I worry about how our lender will treat us in the spring.*

*My wife and I are so busy - we don't have time to talk. When we do, we argue. She's been a real trooper, but I'm afraid she's losing patience with farming.*

*To her, long hours and stress are manageable if we actually are getting ahead. It hardly seems worth it to her anymore. The financial problems are bad enough, but I'm really starting to get scared about us.*

While this excerpt is a fictional dialogue, it reflects a reality many farm families are facing. The farmer briefly outlines a major drama unfolding in his life. He describes how the weather has impacted his life, his wife's feelings and what this all might mean. A summary like this requires prior thought and emotional work.

In their 1990 book, "Interpersonal Accounts," psychologists John Harvey, Terri Orbuch and Ann Weber explain how reconstructing past events with emotions and meanings is vital to recovery from trauma. They feel that whether the trauma involves death, injury, divorce, financial loss, abuse or betrayal, recovery depends on account-making and confiding one's story to others.

An account is a personal story about the cause of the trauma and how it affected the victim. It contains emotional expressions about one's personality. It includes descriptions of other people and the world.

**Reactions to trauma.** The initial reaction to trauma is shock, numbness and feeling overwhelmed. This is followed by expressions of panic, exhaustion, despair and hopelessness. Denial in the form of escapism, avoidance and isolation follows.

For a brief time after.the loss, denial may be a natural and useful coping mechanism. However, if a person continues to engage in denial or avoids or distracts him or herself from dealing with the issue, there is no significant movement toward recovery.

After denial comes the stage of intrusion. The trauma victim is beset by intense obsessional thoughts or images of the loss. Victims worry about what will happen to them because of the loss. They have to gain control over intrusive thoughts. The loss is faced directly and the search for meaning begins.

**Sharing the pain.** It is in the denial and intrusion stages that the victim begins to try out the rudiments of their story of what happened with a trusted confidant.

It takes courage to face the pain - to verbally confide confusion, fear, anger and hurt. It is a big step. How the story, is received makes a big difference. If early attempts at confiding are rebuffed or received without empathy, the trauma victim retreats to an earlier stage such as avoidance or denial.

If the confidant listens well, offers feedback and is there when the victim needs to talk, the victim's account of the tragedy continues to develop. The victim intensifies his or her effort to understand the event and to tell a complete story.

Research has shown that people who confide - write in a diary, share with a spouse, confide in close friends, or participate in a support group - show greater and quicker recovery than those who do not. Failure to work through the account often results in psychosomatic complaints, prolonged grief and anxiety, and difficulty in coping.

**Completing the story.** The final stages of recovery occur when the victim completes their understanding about what happened and why. The traumatic event has forced a change of identity that includes the loss. Feelings of completion of the story and of acceptance of the loss are vital to recovery.

In going through the process of recovery, the trauma victim develops an increased sense of control over their thoughts and feelings about the loss. They are willing to feel the pain of the loss.

They sense having gained skill in coping and being in control again. Their story can be told without great anguish. Part of the healing process is the need to tell others about what one has learned about loss, pain, hope and meaning. Survivors tell their truths again and again to make their experience valuable to others. The story of indomitable human spirit is passed on as a beacon of hope to any who have to go through a similar journey.

# Taking Control Of Our Lives

Life can be overwhelming. Unhappiness takes many forms. Debt robs us of our time and ease. Conflict in close relationships leaves us lonely and upset. Life without challenging and meaningful work is empty and directionless. Time pressure adds layers of stress to what would normally be pleasurable and good.

How can we take control of our lives? What is our vision of the ideal life? Or do we flow with the circumstances of life? Does the bombardment of materialistic images and enticements put us on a treadmill with no end? How much entertainment and leisure do we really need to leaven our day?

Consider these five points.

**1. Sound personal finance brings freedom.** Avoid debt. Budget. Live within your budget. Spend less than you make or find a way to bring in more income.

If we are successful in creating a healthy relationship between income and expenses, then the challenge becomes one of preventing our wants from becoming our needs. No matter what our income, it seems our expenses will rise to the same or a higher level.

Savings and investments are storehouses of future time. Wealth is stored time. Debt is a mortgage on your future time. The struggle to survive economically involves a commitment of your time and energy. First survive, then thrive. Once you've crossed the threshold of meeting basic needs, use your means to do good and free your time to follow your own agenda for life.

**2. Live life with purpose.** Know what you want and why. In the grander scheme of things, our lives have to mean something. Our goals sustain us. We need a noble cause. We have talent to express, contributions to make and energy to apply to problems of our own choosing.

Our workday is a structured centerpiece of our lives. We need work that gives an appropriate level of challenge and stretches human talent and capacity. We should be involved to the point where we get lost in the flow of time and work. Life doesn't give its best rewards to the lazy. Sacrifice precedes success.

**3. Learn to nurture loving relationships.** Work has the capacity to crowd out time and attention for another aspect of happiness - human relationships. Life is about love and seeking the happiness of a mate in marriage. It's about rearing and enjoying family life with children. It's about sharing with friends and family the joys and struggles of life's journey.

We need intimacy and sharing. We need to feel connected and in harmony with those around us. We need to give freely of ourselves with little thought to ourselves. Love creates love. The love we give and the good we do will surely come back to us. We do not need to seek it, demand it or expect it.

Too few of us experiment with how service brings happiness

- both to others and ourselves. Pay attention to the needs of others. Get outside of oneself. Give the gift of service to things that really matter - to those you love, to the stranger, to the less fortunate and the community.

**4. Find and put God in your life.** We have a need to understand life and who we are. We need to make sense of the world. We need to grapple with justice and injustice, good and evil, right and wrong and to settle on rules for living well and happy. To feel good about ourselves, we have to live up to the truth we know and understand.

We need strength and courage for times of adversity and loss. There are times when spiritual peace and understanding can only come from above. Our understanding of God's love for us gives us faith to withstand the trails of life.

The world has many enticements, distractions and counterfeit gods that give pleasure but do not satisfy the soul. Our journey in life is short-sighted if we do not look to a greater power than ourselves. The truths we find challenge us to become better than we are and to fulfill our earthly potential.

There is a practical side to spiritual commitment. It offers a buffer to stress, a network of supportive friends, and the meaning and skills for coping with crisis. Being a regular church attender can protect us from destructive lifestyle problems - drinking, smoking, divorce, delinquency, suicide and even some forms of mental illness.

**5. Cultivate optimism and a positive attitude.** Our mind is a powerful tool. If we examine our basic assumptions about life, we can shape our outlook and feelings. Life is good. Other people are basically good. We are good. We can trust in God and in the course of life.

Optimism helps us to take reasonable risks. Setbacks are lessons to be learned. Mistakes help us grow. Failure is a stepping stone to a future success. Grief and loss are the price we pay for loving and caring deeply.

A sense of humor, an ability to laugh at ourselves and life, is a saving grace. It puts distance between us and the problem. It is a gift to be able to detach from pressing problems by putting them in a positive light, by spiritual understanding or by laughing at their lack of power over us.

Have some fun. Laugh with your friends. Lighten up. As serious as life may be, we help ourselves when we don't take ourselves or life too seriously.

# Humor Vital As A Coping Tool

**Humor and suicide.** Charles Dickens wrote a little fanciful tale about the visit of a little man to a baron suffering from despondency. He introduced himself to the baron as the "Genius of Despair and Suicide." He immediately began to persuade the baron to kill himself.

At one point in the conversation, the baron laughed. This disturbed the "Genius." He asked the baron to sigh, not to laugh. Later on, the baron gave a hearty laugh. The spirit of suicide uttered a frightful howl and disappeared.

There's also the story about an old man who was walking down a country road carrying a huge load of wood on his back. Feeling overwhelmed by his burden, he cast it to the ground and cried out, *"I can't take it anymore. Let the Angel of Death come and take me."* At this, the Angel of Death appeared and asked, *"You called?"* The old man looked at him. *"Yes,"* he said, *"Would you help me get this load back on my shoulders?"*

**Humor and adversity.** T.W. Higginson said, *"There is no defense against adverse fortune which is, on the whole, as effectual as a habitual sense of humor."*

Sometimes the only way to bear a burden is to laugh at them and bear them anyway. Life is hard, but without laughter, it appears intolerable. Sometimes the only choice seems to be between laughter and tears.

There was a time when my wife and I experienced an incredible series of misfortunes. We made a list. The list became so long we laughed and delighted to remember other things to add to the list. It became hilarious. Somehow, laughing about it magically made the pain bearable. Those events were never as painful again.

*"Laughing or crying is what a human being does when there is nothing else to do. The biggest laughs are based on the biggest disappointments and biggest fears."* -Kurt Vonnegut.

**Laughter tells us we belong.** One of the pleasures of belonging to a support group is the unexpected laughter one finds there. As participants recount their struggles or losses, they see the humor in precisely the same way. Humor defuses their anger. Humor heals their pain.

*"Conversation never sits easier than when we now and then discharge ourselves in a symphony of laughter."* - Sir Richard Steele.

Emotions such as hate, fear, panic, despair and frustration incapacitate the body. Positive states of mind such as love, faith, hope, laughter, determination, purpose and perseverance mobilize the body toward health.

Behavioral immunology has confirmed the connection between immunity and the mind. Deep and sustained laughter releases endorphins that actually block pain. The statement, "If it didn't hurt so much I could laugh," is transformed to, "If I didn't laugh about it, it would hurt too much."

*"For health and the constant enjoyment of life, give me a keen sense of humor: it is the next best thing to an abiding faith in providence."* - G.B. Cheever.

Experts have found that high levels of stress precede illness. Thus, control over stressful events is important. Good health depends on control over stressful events. Even the illusion of control helps generate antibodies to fight disease.

Even when actual events are beyond our control, the only control we have left is our attitude and reaction to those events. Laughter is a way of expressing, despite everything, that the distressing events haven't got the best of us yet.

*"With the fearful strain that is on me night and day, if I did not laugh, I should die."* - Abraham Lincoln.

**The situation may be hopeless but it is not serious.** Humor is the evidence of our freedom - the freedom to transform our pain, anxieties and circumstances into absurdities. We choose to accept the painful reality the way it is and laugh at it instead of lamenting about how unjust it may be.

*"A man isn't poor if he can still laugh."* - Raymond Hitchcock.

Laughter shows the deep realization that we are bigger than our troubles, that we are not doomed to live a sorry future after all. Tragedy becomes melodrama and melodrama becomes comedy.

*"I don't think you can truly be funny unless there has been some suffering."* - Carol Burnett.

The gravity by which some people view their troubles often comes from a misplaced sense of pride or dignity. People who can laugh at themselves and their mistakes have disarmed their worst critic themselves. Laughing at oneself shows deep self-acceptance and takes away the threat of humiliation or embarrassment from others. By poking fun at our self-importance, we take the sting from our errors.

*"If it is with outer seriousness, it must be with inner humor. If it is with outer humor, it must be with inner seriousness. Neither one alone without the other will do."* - Robert Frost.

**How important is a sense of humor?** Charles Lindner had an answer. *"A person has two legs and one sense of humor, and if you're faced with the choice, it is better to lose a leg."*

# Farm Crisis Has A Silver Lining

If we live long enough, we will experience the heart-wrenching cry of the soul when the unthinkable happens. The world is turned upside down. Everything changes.

Facing the threat and uncertainty of losing a farm and working through a financial crisis challenges fundamental coping skills of farmers. Even more challenging is losing the farm and having to rethink one's occupation and place to live. This is a huge loss and a threat to a farmer's self-confidence, identity and even hope.

This is new territory. There are no guarantees people in crisis will cope well. Farmers go through denial, anger, bitterness, confusion, withdrawal, anxiety, and depression. Marital problems are common. The pain and misery can be overwhelming. It seems as though life can never be good again.

What good can come from such a life crisis? This is a crisis that disrupts relationships, burdens the soul with grief, challenges basic values and beliefs and places powerful demands on people to adapt to unwanted circumstances.

For farm families, here are ten life changing attitudes and skills that develop from coping well with a life crisis.

**1. Turning to a confidant for support.** During a crisis, farmers share their private thoughts, fears and desires with a trusted friend, relatives or spouse. By turning to others, deeper and more meaningful relationships are promoted.

**2. Developing better relationships with family and friends.** The crisis brings out vulnerability, dependency and isolation. Farmers have to rely on others and engage with them in joint problem solving to meet everyone's needs. They come to understand how important family and friends are and how important it is to communicate openly with them.

**3. Forming new social networks.** Farmers reach out to counselors, clergy, self-help groups and other informal sources of support to learn about the predicament they are in and to find purpose and meaning in what they are going through. New friendships are made. Social support helps people know they are cared about and understood.

**4. Going to a deeper level of understanding.** The crisis compels farmers to take a broader view of the world. The old way of looking at life isn't sufficient. Farmers are pushed and stretched into finding deeper levels of understanding and finding new ideas and meanings to help them cope. They often find peace through greater spiritual understanding and faith.

**5. Acquiring more self-reliance and self-understanding.** New circumstances force farmers into unfamiliar roles and new, seemingly overwhelming tasks. As they measure up to new demands, they develop new self-appreciation and become self-confident. Once they have successfully dealt with the crisis, they then have a new capacity to take life in stride. They become more easygoing and self-confident in dealing with new obstacles in their path.

**6. Growing with greater empathy, altruism and maturity.** Crisis exposes farmers to others with similar problems. They become more sensitive to others' needs and feelings. They learn compassion. They see the need to reach out and help others. They assume new roles and responsibilities that benefit the community and the welfare of others. They become better neighbors. They become less judgmental.

**7. Realigning basic values and priorities.** The crisis may cause farmers to question their values and rethink their goals and priorities. Life is short. The really important things become obvious. They realign their goals with their new sense of what life is all about.

**8. Developing new problem-solving skills.** Farmers come to see their new situation as a challenge. They begin to analyze their new difficulties logically and take positive steps and actions to manage the crisis. They push themselves to understand the problem, find meaning in it and redefine the situation in a larger and more hopeful context.

**9. Choosing to seek help.** Farmers seek information and resources to manage the crisis. They know they don't know enough and reach out to others for help. Seeking help is a turning point in positive coping.

**10. Gaining a greater ability to manage and regulate emotions.** Life hasn't prepared some farmers for the intense tumult of emotions that accompany a life crisis. In order to cope, they learn to bring their emotions under control so they can get on with solving their problems. Emotions expressed inappropriately can harm important relationships and hinder effective problem-solving.

Farmers can emerge from a crisis with additional coping skills and closer relationships with family and friends. There are new priorities, with greater self-understanding and maturity and a richer appreciation of life. A life crisis can make us more resilient, tender and humble.

Life is full of inspiring stories about how the indomitable human spirit shines through the most dire of circumstances. When life takes a measure of us, we need to measure up. Someday, in less painful circumstances, we will acknowledge the good and the growth that came from going through something hard.

This list of ten ways of growing from a life crisis was adapted from the research findings of health research scientist Jeanne Schaefer and psychologist Rudolf Moos at the Stanford University Medical Center in Palo Alto, California.

# Which Is It? Go To Plan B Or Get A Grip?

In the middle of the night in May 1998, I was listening to the sound of death. It was the rumble of distant thunder. It was the sound of rain falling. These were my thoughts as I pondered the situation.

Why is a life-giving force such as rain so menacing? Instead of nourishing the soil, it is nourishing dark, runaway thoughts as farmers listen to the sounds. This sound of death is the death of family farms. Dark thoughts, growing with each storm, are thoughts about quitting farming, quitting while there is something left.

In eastern North Dakota and northwestern Minnesota farmers are being drowned out again, little by little. I should say "a lot by a lot" as storm after incessant storm passes through the region. The water comes on the heels of last years flooding and blizzards. Too much water.

In Texas, it is too little water for farmers and ranchers. Here it is diseased crops. Too many weeds. More work. More spraying. More expense. More waiting to get into the fields. More worry. Record low prices. Poorer yields. More problems for next year.

Normally decisive farmers and ranchers, as confident and sure-footed as battle hardened generals, begin to second guess themselves. How sad that farmers who chose to spend a delightfully sunny Fourth of July with their families berate themselves the next day for not working on the holiday. Unexpected heavy rains stops their spraying! Is this what rural living has come to? Does life have to be this tense?

**Does Michael Jordan quit at the top of his game?** Unless he is as rare as Rocky Marciano or Jim Brown, he doesn't. People don't quit on a good year. It is too tempting to go another round - to have one more crowning success.

Smart farmers and ranchers, hard working rural families, people who have been consistently ahead of the curve in their business decisions, those as normally optimistic as the bright sunshine, the "Michael Jordan" kind of people - are planning their departure from agriculture. They are the harbingers of things to come.

Like everything else they have done, they are good at separating emotion from business decisions. They look ahead and decide to move to something else. They are not ready to let all that they have worked for go down the drain. They have nothing left to prove, either to themselves or to their neighbors.

They are at a crossroads. This year will be perfect for buying land. Others will be leaving out of necessity. To expand and grow is the way to stay in the game. But what is it all for? They have their retirement secure already. They can live well and choose their new way of life while they have their security in hand.

Why take on additional risks? Why add stress of new payments, more work, more equipment while sacrificing more family time? Goals have driven them. The hard weather years have made them realize that they have already accomplished all they need to accomplish. Work has stopped being fun and they know it.

Now is the time to go to plan B. Or invent plan B. They do not leave agriculture in shame but look at their lives with the same analytical powers they use on their farming and ranching decisions. Their decision to quit while ahead will someday look really good to others who find out they chose to stay too long.

**But what about farmers and ranchers who still have future goals?** What are they supposed to think about this year or last or about the general trends in agriculture? Their goals are not for themselves but for their way of life and for the family farm or ranch being passed on to a son or daughter who already has the soil in their blood. They have plenty of incentive to stay.

They are being overwhelmed by the stress and worry of events slipping out of their control. Weather is one enemy that is tough to beat. The markets are another.

This will be a good year if they regain their nerve. Their enemy, an unfamiliar one, is stress. They are not used to having their decisions go haywire - to losing when they should be winning.

It will be a good year if they learn they are human, that they are not perfect and that their focus is too narrow. It will be a good year if they learn to rally around each other, figure out what is really important and to live with the bad as well as the good.

For them, success has come naturally. Now it is time to become acquainted with surviving really tough years. Conditions will change. There is a future in agriculture. Good years will return. Weather will be favorable. They will be positioned to take advantage of the great rewards in agriculture to be had for those still in the game.

It is persistence, determination and faith that sustain people when all else fails. It is clarity of purpose. This isn't the year Karl Malone and John Stockton quit either. It is enjoying the struggle. It is knowing how good you really are and being willing to make another run at the top.

This is a testing year. Same farmers and ranchers, same abilities - different decisions. They are smart. They know something isn't right and they are taking corrective action now. Go to Plan B or get a grip - or both.

# Honey, I Shrunk The Farm

In the winter of 1999, I was privileged to help organize three retreats for farm couples. The funding was provided by the MeritCare Foundation. Two retreats were for farmers facing economic and emotional stress due to the farm economy. The third retreat was for farm couples who had made the decision to quit farming.

Fifty-four farm couples participated. We had pretest and post test measures for the retreat plus we planned a 6-month follow up. At the end of the retreat couples gave feedback on what they got from the retreat. Here is what they said.

**1. All were in the same boat.** They appreciated being around other farm couples who were in the same situation. This was the best and most powerful factor. They were away from their local community and could talk freely about their feelings and situation and feel deeply understood by their fellow farmers. You can't imagine how healing this was. For the couples leaving farming, this was an overwhelming aspect of the retreat they appreciated the most.

The farm couples formed new relationships, talked openly and honestly about their lives, shared tears and laughter. We had numerous small group discussions mixed in with the presentations and an entertainment program. We had family style meals and plenty of chances where everyone could mingle on a one-to-one basis. They heard each others' stories and concerns, and inspired each other to resolve to cope with their problems.

At the end, each group wanted a reunion retreat to further be accountable and to renew their associations with each other.

**2. Couple communication.** We had a graphic "hands on" demonstration of how conflict conversations could be handled using a speaker/listener technique. We had volunteers - graduate students in marriage and family therapy from North Dakota State University - to help "coach" each couple on how to implement the principles involved. It worked! Many couples appreciated the new tools they were given and resolved to go back home and work on improving their communication.

Also, many couples decided to make major improvements in their relationships. They were going to put more priority on their marriage, appreciate one another more, be more loving, be more supportive and work through problems together. Their coming to the retreat as a couple strengthened marriages. They enjoyed the time away together and the time to talk through the things they were learning, thinking and feeling.

For part of the program we had couples work together, also with coaching assistance, on developing a "vision" statement for their lives. This helped them focus on their values and the purpose of their lives. It will help them work on the big picture instead of being drowned with their day-to-day problems.

**3. Stress management.** We had presentations on depression, anxiety, stress management, grief and loss, helping children with the farm crisis, humor, plus some quality entertainment and an ecumenical religious service on faith and hope. Each couple took away something different, something they needed.

They resolved to manage their stress better and knew better how to do it. One farmer said, "I've learned to be more optimistic about life even if the situation in farming is negative." Another reflected, "Honey, I shrunk the farm!"

A humorist helped the couples loosen up. They laughed at some of their problems for the first time in a long time. They played. They sang around a bonfire. We had a farmer and ex-farmer present musical programs that touched their hearts and their lifestyle. The couples resolved to go home and to bring humor and laughter back into their lives.

We had an inspirational speaker, Lowell Nelson, who told his story of how his farming career ended. Lowell's honest and compelling message made a big impression. He reminded them of what was really important in life and how to put the farm crisis in perspective. By the end of the retreat, many had specific action plans to face their problems head on rather than to be stuck in their misery.

**4. Technical advice.** We had a couple of presentations on different aspects of debt and the legal issues connected with farming. These were well received. We had a presentation by our state's Job Service on employment issues. For the first two retreats, we had a program on farm management options in today's down economy. There were some concrete decisions our farm couples needed to make to get back in control of their lives. For some, this was what they needed to know.

Does this sound good? Judging by the reaction of the participants, some of who were initially skeptical and fearful, it exceeded their expectations. To me, now a veteran of two farm crises and prominent advice giver for farmers on stress and coping, this was the most effective way I've seen of helping farmers in distress. The retreat brought them hope, new ideas, new friends, skills and the courage to move on with their lives.

# When All Else Fails, Lighten Up!

A publisher asked the Canadian psychologist, Hans Selye, to provide a one page summary of his path breaking book on stress and the General Adaptation Syndrome, the flight or fight response of our body when exposed to stress. He did so and he also suggested the serenity prayer as a one paragraph summary of his work.

*"Lord, grant me the serenity to accept the things I cannot change, the courage to change the things I can and the wisdom to know the difference."* - St. Francis of Assisi.

Selye then added a two-word summary of his book and also the serenity prayer - "Lighten up."

**A humorist does her thing.** I observed the application of this theory first hand during the three-day retreats for farm couples struggling with the farm economy and the changes it meant in their lives. A humorist was part of an evening entertainment program. She was a lot of fun and really got the group to laugh, play and be silly. It was good-hearted fun.

As the retreats progressed and as people got to know each other's personalities, the fun and hilarity picked up. Laughter came easily and the people drew closer together. One evening several individuals plunged in an ice-covered lake as a part of their playfulness. Brrrr! Crazy! Good fun! You bet!

As the couples evaluated the retreat experience, I was struck how many of them commented on the humorist, the fun and her message about the importance of humor and coping. There were many beneficial aspects of the retreats but I was surprised at how powerful humor was rated as one of the valuable experiences the participants took home with them. Many resolved that they were going to laugh and play with each other, with their children, and lighten up their approach to life and their troubles.

I find that support groups often quickly move from tears to laughter and then back and forth again. Seeing the world in the same way means you laugh deeply at the same things. It helps people feel they belong. They feel understood.

**Humor and detachment.** People who have a sense of humor have an edge when it comes to the setbacks, disappointments, absurdities and even the tragedies of life. Having a sense of humor shows an ability to detach and take a bigger view of a situation than its oppressive qualities. If we can't change it, we can laugh at it. It may be tough, but our laughter shows we are not yet defeated.

During the farm crisis of the mid-80s a couple in a support group commented on another couple, friends who were hurting badly. They felt they could gauge when their friends entered into their black pit by when they lost their sense of humor. They could also tell when they were over the worst of it by when they got their sense of humor back.

**Can you come out and play?** Mark Twain said, *"Work consists of whatever a body is obliged to do, and play consists of whatever a body is not obliged to do."* Play is a child's work. It is a miniature world of safety where children experiment, rehearse, practice skills and resolve conflict. Play is the ability to shift concentration, exchange roles, and step outside of oneself. Time is set aside to observe, pretend, enjoy or create. The world gets bigger through play.

A playful attitude can help us meet life's challenges. Life, viewed as a game, has no consequence severe enough to defeat us, no failure that is not a stepping stone in disguise, no experience from which we cannot learn.

It is fun to see adults play. Play introduces us to that little boy or girl inside of us who looks wide-eyed at life with wonder and curiosity. We see the complexity and the contradiction. A fascination with the unevenness of life balances and softens our straight ahead struggle with problems and challenges.

**Where does play and humor fit in?** We can't neglect the basics of life: doing our duty, gaining spiritual understanding, meeting the challenges of life, having integrity and moral sensitivity, and giving service to others. However, life doesn't have to be an endless series of chores that are to be crossed off a list with a heavy sigh. Life doesn't need to be grim, serious, or tedious.

Having play in our lives doesn't mean being idle and irresponsible, buying pleasure or engaging in aimless activity. It does not have to be a big weekend, a magnificent vacation or a grand escape. It is merely an investment of time and energy in the unobligated parts of life - "wasting" time on activities that don't directly add up but count nevertheless.

Through play in parenting, needs are met. Through fun in the family, memories are created. Through play and fun in marriage, love is expressed. Through play, friendships are deepened. Through play and fun in living, we maintain our sanity, our perspective and our strength.

What a healthy, wholesome thing it was to see adults play and laugh together! I almost see the clouds of depression lift as people let go of their worries and enjoyed the moment. Hans Selye and St. Francis were onto something - maybe I should've jumped in that lake too!

*CHAPTER FOUR*

# FAMILIES GOING THROUGH IT TOGETHER

## Farm Women React To Financial Stress

*Here is an insightful letter I received from a farm woman describing the emotional plight of some of the women in her farming community.*

Dear Dr. Farmer,

I am writing you to express myself about a farming issue that weighs heavily on my shoulders. I know I am not alone. I have admired your column for years and have been amazed on how "right on" it is on farming issues as they affect relationships.

First, I want to say that our marriage is very sound. In fact, we happen to be best friends and confidantes more than anything. Secondly, I want to say that if anything can test that relationship, it is the trials and tribulations of trying to figure out the farm mess; get in, stay in— keep on trying, it will get better, how to pay taxes if we get out, what will dad say about the farm. It goes on and on. In our area it's utterly amazing how many people are dropping out. To say it is an epidemic is not too drastic.

I feel there is a forgotten group out there that suffers as much as the farmer and that is the spouse. Many women have talked with me. I know about their feelings of pain and what is happening with their family. I can pinpoint some of the common things I hear and, to some degree, feel myself.

1. **A feeling of being left out of the loop.** Many times the wife doesn't know until that terrible time when the husband gets the final bad luck at the bank in February or March just how bad it really is. Their husbands have been non-communicative about the details of the financial crunch. Only when confronted with options that spell disaster - incredible IRS numbers, facing new employment, selling the land - do some women find out the truth. When this happens, the next problem arises.

2. **A feeling of being inadequate to address their husband's emotional hurt and feeling her pain is not being treated seriously.** Many of the women describe their farming spouse as having been taciturn, remote, and unable to share his emotions. Even the sharing of bad news comes in bits and pieces.

   The wife often feels her husband is depressed, lonely, and won't seek help from loved ones or neighbors because of feelings of shame and inadequacy. This is a new ballgame for her and she asks herself, "What do I do?" "Is it O.K. to talk about this with someone or will he be mad?" "Do I dare bring this up today or is it better to let him deal with it alone?"

   The problem with all this is that often times the woman has her own emotional needs that have to be met by someone during the crisis.

3. **A sense of fear.** Most farm women now work off the farm. When faced with the fact that her husband may be getting out, she often feels fearful that her income will have to suffice - and she knows it won't.

   Also, many of these women blindly signed farm notes for chattels and operations. She is scared she will be financially on the hook at some point in time. She is scared, not just for her and the children, but for him too. He may be facing finding a new occupation at 40, 50 or 60.

4.  **A feeling of confusion.** "How did this happen?" "I don't understand it." No one really sat down with her and explained the cost of production. No one explained the financial package they have. No one explained how much equity in the land they are losing and how.

5.  **Feelings of being mad and resentful.** Perhaps this one is the hardest for women to talk about - that somewhere inside of them they **are** mad that this has happened. They are mad at their husband for not keeping them informed. They are mad that the bank never explained their personal liability. The women I talk to feel guilty about being mad!!

Well, Dr Farmer, these are just some thoughts I have about this crazy mess the farm community is in. I personally try to stay positive and that is not always easy to do. For us, we are continuing on. Only the future will tell us if we have made a mistake or if we have been wise.

Sometimes I think a spouse support group would be warranted. I am not sure the farmers would want anyone to know their business though!! They are tough nuts to crack, like the saying goes. Thank you for listening. - - A northwestern Minnesota farm woman.

# Cowboys Don't Cry
# And They Don't Talk Either

During the fall of 1997, I gave several presentations on stress and coping in the ranch country of Northwestern and North Central South Dakota. These ranchers were anything but jòlly.

They had undergone the worst winter in their memory. They faced a seemingly unending series of killer blizzards, life threatening cold and wind chills, and paralyzing deep concrete-like snows. The winter began early and ended late with the worst blizzard occurring at the peak of spring calving season.

At times these ranchers were helpless to protect and feed their livestock. They lost control. Mother Nature was too furious and too powerful. Cattle herds were devastated with unprecedented death loss, calving losses and reproductive difficulties. People in this country take their responsibility to care for the animals personally. For some, their losses meant a financial wreck for the year and grave worry about financial survival.

**Emotions ran high.** Men and women were feeling fatigue, anger, guilt, fear, depression, despair, panic, anxiety and isolation. The drain of worry, preoccupation, stress-induced irritability and blame tested their relationships. People were driven stir crazy by the school children at home and their inability to leave and see other people.

It wasn't all negative as neighbors helped neighbors when they could. Families pulled together and enjoyed their enforced togetherness. Couples learned to appreciate each other's heroic gutsiness and courage as they dealt with incredible adversity.

Men and women handled the isolation differently. For women, the phone was a lifeline. They checked on one another and experienced the relief of sharing their feelings, concerns and losses. Talking about their difficulties and emotions came as easily as a flood swollen stream running down hill.

As we discussed the trauma of the winter, the most frequent question was about how men handle strong emotion. Male frustration came out often in the form of blame and anger - emotions to which many men in agriculture give free rein. Of more concern however, was how men bottled up their feelings and retreated into the privacy of their own thoughts and worries.

**These are tough people, independent to a fault.** The men have learned a rigid code of masculinity - hiding weakness and fear, being stoic and uncomplaining about problems and solving one's problems by oneself. They did not open themselves up to receive love and support from those closest to them nor did they offer much of a listening ear or an understanding heart.

This code of heroic self-sufficiency works well in tough ranch country but when a man loses control in a prolonged crisis, his normal coping skills are overwhelmed. His virtues become a liability.

**The key to coping is talking.** By talking openly, a man can invite the care and love of others into his life, have a sounding board to sort through his emotional turmoil, and engage his problem-solving response to solve dilemmas. By sharing the unknown, he starts down a path of gathering strength, resources and information and putting things into perspective.

There is one more thing. Fear and feelings of inadequacy blind him to the fact that his wife is in crisis also. What does she need? Her psychological makeup is grounded in a need to feel connected. Emotional isolation feels terrible. Her husband's emotional withdrawal drives her crazy. She takes on a double burden - her own stress plus worry about her husband's coping ability.

Ranch women complain they are left alone with their own fears and need for support. They have a need to talk things out in order to understand. Being traditional females, they are denied their opportunity to comfort, nurture and soothe their husband. It creates doubt and frustration about their identity as a loving marriage partner. "If you can't even get close and support one another during a time of crisis, then what is this marriage all about?"

Some women become angry when their men refuse to talk about their distress. They find this lack of closeness difficult to share with others because it is so personal. It reflects on their adequacy as a female.

**She is lonely - lonely for the togetherness that marriage is supposed to provide.** She wants to cry out for help, for attention, for someone to take care of her, for someone to share the trauma of what is happening to herself and her family. She has to be strong for others and strong in a crisis. It would help so much if she could be nurtured in turn.

There are two lonely people. The other is her tough hyper-masculine husband. He chooses his loneliness out of a misguided sense of always needing to be strong and finding solutions by himself.

What a man needs during a time of crisis is to get back in control. Having a confidante and turning to others for help is the quickest and best avenue to recovery. A woman needs the same thing. She also needs to feel connected, loved and confident about her primary relationships.

The best thing a man can do for a woman in a time of crisis is to offer her the emotional support she craves. Doing this is simple - talk and listen. He plays the key role in relieving her trauma and setting in motion her coping skills. It is a manly thing to do.

# Marital Support During A Time Of Crisis

I met with a group of farmers and their spouses in Langdon, North Dakota that were seeking more information about coping skills for tough times. During one part of the program, men and women split into separate discussion groups to consider the question, "What do men/women want from their spouses during a time of crisis?

The conclusions they made were instructive and helpful as a springboard for other couples to discuss their own personal relationships.

**What farmers want from their wives:**
1. **Understand your husbands' duties and pressures.** Work on the farm involves more than driving a tractor or combine. Paperwork and reading have to be done on rainy days. Farmers need to keep abreast of markets and governmental regulations. They feel the need to keep up with weather and politics. Knowledgeable discussion and support on these matters help.

2. **Help keep the finances under control.** The grain check has to pay for production costs and other bills. Even though there may be money in the bank, it is accounted for. They want their wives to accompany them to see the lender for major negotiations.

3. **Learn about the big picture.** They also talked about their wives needing to see the big picture and understanding the long term investments related to farming. Many of the decisions a farmer makes today affects the future.

   The farmers in the group acknowledged that farmers may keep concerns to themselves. As a result, they carry a large burden of stress. They recognize their own role in not sharing their feelings about what certain decisions mean.

4. **Communicate more about financial, social and spiritual concerns.** They want their wives to "walk" with them, be together in decisions, be open, be mutually helpful with duties, and provide a loving and supportive home environment. During a time of crisis, these farmers see a need to simplify life, back off on activities and look for emotional support.

5. **Encourage good mental attitudes and spiritual strength.** Men recognized the need to be alert for signs of depression. They discussed the natural tendency to feel sorry for oneself and their need to develop a hopeful attitude. They saw the time of crisis as a time when they, as a couple, come to God. If there is a tug of war, they want their wives to remember they are on the same, not opposite, sides.

**What farm women want from their husbands:**

1. **Share the big picture.** They want to know the big picture even though they may not want to know the details. Too much knowledge is scary, burdensome and not healthy. A woman has a host of other concerns keeping up as a "mother" and paying attention to other relationships. Also, when a wife learns the depth of a problem she may spend more time worrying. This may distract her from her other responsibilities.

It's embarrassing to be questioned about farm plans and changes from friends and neighbors and not have a clue.

If the woman is the bookkeeper for the operation, financial reality can be pretty scary. She wants to share this information with her husband and sense his openness in dealing with problems. Denial or avoidance leaves her alone with a painful reality she can't share.

2. **Show respect.** It is a sign of respect to take the time to fill their wives in on the significant developments and farm decisions being made. The husband should respect and be willing to consider his wife's opinion and be influenced by her.

She needs emotional support and a sounding board just like he does. Men need to detach enough from their own concerns and worry to show empathy and concern for their wives' lives.

3. **Let me let go.** "If it is his responsibility, I have to let go and trust him." There may be a division of roles that works efficiently for the family and the farm. Becoming too involved, especially when the involvement isn't appreciated, can drive a wedge between the couple.

4. **Make spiritual activity a priority.** The women discussed the need to pray as a couple. There was a lot of concern expressed about Sundays not being a day of rest and worship. They wanted their husbands to take responsibility to help bring God into their relationship. The man of the family leading the family is a good example and practice for the family.

5. **Support involvement in the community.** Staying involved socially and maintaining friendships are important. So is community service. By connecting with the community the couple keeps their problems in perspective. It will take their mind off their own troubles so they can experience the joys of giving to others.

It was remarkable that men and women were essentially saying the same thing. "We need to go through this together."

# Dealing With Differences During A Time Of Crisis

Farm couples have to communicate deeply about goals and the daunting problems they face. They need to offer comfort and encouragement as each in their own way seeks to cope with their raw emotion, confusion and hurt.

A crisis highlights important differences in attitude and perspective about how to deal with problems. If these differences are handled in a good way, each partner will feel supported and cared for despite their struggle to find a mutual strategy for survival. Here are some important differences that are especially challenging during hard times.

**Desire to communicate.** One partner needs to talk and share details and emotion about what is happening in their lives. The other partner may not see the importance in talking about events or emotions. In those situations where couples clash about their communication styles, about 90 percent of the time it is the wife who wants more conversation and emotional intimacy while 10 percent of the time it is the husband who is frustrated.

During times of crisis, the need to communicate at a deep level becomes an important coping tool. Husbands as well as wives want their spouse to be "there" for them, be together in decisions, talk openly, give each other mutual respect and provide a loving and supportive home environment.

**Allocation of time**. Couples need to have a shared understanding about their duties and responsibilities. Important differences occur around how much time is devoted to farming and how much time is devoted to relationships, time within the home, leisure and family traditions and rituals.

Some men are more driven by work and their need to keep up with other aspects of farming, - for example - markets, technology, weather, farm records and governmental regulations. It is easy to feel overwhelmed and preoccupied. On the other hand, farm women may be more conscious of fitting in time to meet important social and emotional needs in the family and to provide a balance for all the work demands of farming.

The couple may have differences in terms of physical and sexual energy, what time of day they are able to connect on a personal basis and even on how much time together is satisfactory. They may differ on how much time is spent with the extended family, socializing with friends, community involvement, entertaining, and how to spend the holidays. Some men may feel a need to simplify life and back off on activities when they are feeling stressed out. For some women, the social outlets provide meaningful relief from stress.

**Roles within the family.** With many husbands and wives engaged in off-farm employment, couples need to negotiate work roles in the home, involvement in childcare, and other responsibilities so that an unfair burden isn't placed on one spouse's shoulders. It's not just the work though; it is an attitude of cooperation and teamwork that counts. It feels good when you work together instead of pulling apart.

**Getting finances under control.** Marriage partners come from different backgrounds when it comes to their anxiety about debt, how frugal to be, and what is a legitimate expense and what is not. Couples need to cooperate on the farm and household budgets. They need to work out their differences on how to meet their financial obligations and try to be flexible and listen to each other's options and alternatives.

It is a sign of respect and equality in a marriage when couples share the big financial picture and make major farm decisions together. Wives do not like being left out of the loop when it comes to the bank, farm plans, key decisions and basic financial information. Both partners need to be open to each other's influence and opinions.

When a husband (usually it's the male) is in denial, withdrawn, stoical and unable to share his thoughts or emotions with his wife, it isolates her and adds to her stress level and feelings of helplessness. She also needs emotional support and a sounding board just like he does. A husband needs to detach enough from his own worries to show empathy and concern for her concerns. In many cases, his wife is the main bookkeeper for the operation and needs her husband's attention and cooperation in dealing with financial problems.

**Spirituality and faith.** Couples need to sort through their differences when it comes to faith and family worship. They need to pray and to worship as a couple. They need to figure out the deeper meaning of life events through a common spiritual perspective. Important differences in this area are frustrating and prevent a deep unity between them.

If farm couples want to go through crisis together and to develop new strengths and closeness as a couple, they will need to develop a generous and accepting attitude about their differences. Each are worthy of respect and understanding as opposed to saying, "the way you are is wrong." A partner's differences are a gift and benefit the marriage.

How couples handle their differences during hard times will make or break them. Get on the same side. Be a team. One day hopefully you'll say, looking back at these days, "We did good work together. When we have to, we can do a lot. It took the two of us but we did it!"

# Off Farm Work Poses Marital Problems

*In the PBS documentary, "The Farmers Wife's," Darrel and Juanita Buschkoetter, work through the dilemma of working off the farm to generate enough money to live and to keep the farm. First Darrel works in a manufacturing job and later for another farmer. Juanita tries a nursing home, cleaning houses and finally goes back to college to get a degree.*

*The off farm work takes a toll on their marriage and forces them to make hard adjustments. Here are some quotations from "The Farmer's Wife" that dramatize the challenge of off farm work from each of their perspective.*

**Juanita**: We always thought by farming that I'd be able to stay home and take care of the kids. I still think that. I know I'm old fashioned but I think that's what is wrong in the country. I think kids need Mom at home, at least during their developing years.

He (Darrel) was the center of everything I did, you know? But it's only natural after you have three kids, try to save a farm operation and try to go to school, you just don't have enough energy for all that.

After Darrel had been working for close to a year or so, he and his Dad especially thought I should've been the one going to work because it was too hard on Darrel working. So I went to work. One of the worst things I hate about working right now is that I have that much less time with the kids. I sometimes feel like the girls [three daughters] and I are growing further apart. It just scares me that they're growing up so fast and once they're gone you can't make up for the time that you missed. You just really have to put a lot more effort into taking time with each one of them. Maybe that's better in a way because it seems like the things we do now mean a whole lot more.

**Darrel:** At home the whole day goes by and it doesn't even seem like an hour. But at work, an hour goes by and seems like two days. Sometimes I can't hardly stand the way the clock goes so slow at work because I guess it's because I don't enjoy doing what I've been doing . . . It's been hell. It's been hard on my marriage. It's been hard bringing the kids up.

If I could make a living out here on the farm, I wouldn't have to be in town during the day trying to bring home enough income to buy groceries. So naturally I could do a better job of farming and I could be a better father, I could be a better husband. It's just been hell.

But now she's out making a living too, and she takes care of a lot of the finances. She actually has just as much control over things as I do. That probably eats on a guy a little bit.

Trying to farm during the night and work all day for someone else, it's worse than a living hell . . . Your body feels like hell all the time. You know they expect you to be a slave and if you can go 100 miles an hour, they still want you to go twice as fast. People are still human beings, you know? Everybody needs some credit for what they're doing. If you're just going to be like a robot and he tells you to do this and he tells you to do that, that's not for me.

With me, having to have an off farm job, it built up a lot of anger inside of me because any human being alive can take so much stress and after a while it catches up with you. The day after I shut the combine off, I went to work for somebody else and did all the hard work and the dirty work, running everyday. I think it just made me go crazy.

In the past when I was working full time I missed a lot with the kids when they were real small because I was never home. When I came home I was so dead tired and I had chores to do yet and farming to do yet.

**Working on a happy ending.** *The Buschkoetters eventually worked through their financial problems so that Darrel could go back to full time farming. After her schooling, Juanita got a better paying job - one that offered a challenge and some flexibility.*

*Darrel regained his confidence.* "After the last couple of years I think I changed quite a bit. I feel more complete than I ever did. I thought if I couldn't farm that it was the end of the world. Sure that's my dream to farm, but if I absolutely had to do something else, I know there are other lives than farming. I want to be someplace on either the management end or making things tick."

# Two Off-Farm Jobs: Are They Worth It?

To keep the family farm and their dream of being full time farmers, farmers and their wives have added full-time jobs to their already busy and stressed lives. Some started working two jobs during the farm crisis years to keep the farm and claw their way back. The most rapid rise in off-farm work has occurred in the past six or seven years.

The Iowa Farm Poll shows that in Iowa in 1989, 29 percent of men and 44 percent of women had off-farm jobs. In 1994 - just five years later - these percentages had risen to 41 percent for men and 58 percent for women. Stress levels have risen during this period.

Instead of a rural roller coaster, a more accurate description for many of these farm families is that of a rural treadmill - working harder to stay even while having their quality of life deteriorate. Rural sociologist Paul Lasley has described this trend, also noted in the Iowa Farm Poll, as, "doing better and feeling worse."

They can never seem to get ahead. Their goal of being full time farmers remains elusively out of reach. Farmers have exited the hog industry because labor intensive work didn't fit with off-farm work. In many cases, they moved to cattle but now they are facing low cattle prices.

Not just one parent is working. In many communities both parents have entered off-farm employment. Rural America is becoming vacant during the daytime. There are latchkey children and childcare concerns. A critical dimension in the fabric of rural life is unraveling - volunteers.

**Adding the third shift.** Author Arlie Hochschild wrote, "Second Shift," in which she described how women have the lion's share of housework and childcare when they return home from work. Someone should write a book entitled, "The Third Shift," to describe the complex lives of farm men and women who have added full-time jobs to their farming and family responsibilities.

The jobs they go to are either low-paying jobs in small rural communities or they are professional type jobs. These professional jobs carry extra levels of stress and work that they bring home with them. They often require evening obligations and away-from-home training requirements. Scheduling and planning are priorities to avoid conflict and confusion.

Low paying jobs don't bring in that much money when you figure in gas, childcare, and convenience foods. Shift work is even worse - especially for childcare options.

**Increased stress loads.** How do you face the farm bookkeeping or chores in the dark and under bad weather conditions when you've already put in a long and stressful day? Mothers of young children have to deal with guilt and worry about their children's development, sick children, and juggling or missing children's activities. People feel guilty about giving up their volunteer service and activities.

Parents are tired and frustrated. They may take it out on each other or on the kids. There is little time left over for a social life. There are fewer occasions for women to get together and offer each other support. Personal time for couples is at a premium.

Now add to the mix the financial pressures of making payments on land, a combine, a tractor or paying back operating loans. The dollar amounts are huge. The stress levels are great. A lot rides on the quality of the crops and livestock and the prices they'll bring - things outside their control. A machinery breakdown can add an extra blow to a cash flow already spread thin.

**Is it worth it?** It is a heavy price to pay to preserve their dream and lifestyle. In fact, one has to wonder if the fabled lifestyle of the family farm is being destroyed by the farm family's last ditch efforts to save it.

Farm couples try to get through the day and live day to day. They hold the farm, marriage and the kids together and that is about it.

Are the sacrifices worth it? Will they ever be able to give up these extra jobs and go back to full-time farming? Farmers and their wives think it but don't dare say it aloud or to each other. The years of hard work have added up. It would be incredibly hard to bow out at this point.

Instead of people facing foreclosure and bankruptcy, they are wearing out under the strain of high stress, incredible work loads and marginal rewards. No wonder they are "doing better and feeling worse."

# How To Help Children During Hard Times

Rand Conger, a sociologist and researcher at Iowa State University, shared some findings about youth and hard times in a rural setting. He sees two main ways children become more at risk for behavioral and emotional problems, school difficulties, and conflict with peers: parental conflict and parental depression.

**Parental conflict.** When parents quarrel and fight, children feel the stress and tension. Children are alarmed and frightened by the intensity of the anger and no foreseeable problem resolution. The security of the family is threatened.

Furthermore, the anger and frustration the parents have with each other spills over into the relationship with their children. They cannot switch easily from being angry and upset with their spouse one minute to being kind, loving and gentle with their child the next.

The parents' threshold for frustration is low. Conflicts arise when the parents' stress reactions are introduced into the parent/child interactions. Children feel distressed when their own relationship with their parents has too much conflict.

**Parental depression.** When a parent is depressed, he or she loses their concentration and becomes preoccupied with worries and emotions. A depressed parent has less energy and isn't as available to give timely attention to the normal ups and downs, stresses and strains of their children's lives.

Children thrive on attention. Resilient children are good at seeking and enlisting the attention and help of at least one functional parent, relative or caring adult mentor. Parents need to pay attention to their children's lives, thrill to their successes, be at their events, and comfort and counsel them when there are problems.

Children, especially teens, need monitoring and supervision. Parents have to set boundaries, enforce family rules and consequences, and monitor their activities, whereabouts and friendships. This is hard enough under normal circumstances, but extremely hard when a parent is depressed.

**Parenting during hard times.** Parents need to be aware that their children's stress is strongly tied to their own stress reactions to the crisis. Also, parents need to monitor their own emotions, serve as sounding boards for each other and get control of their reactions.

They can seek help for depression and anxiety. Parents need to first reach out and get the emotional support and guidance they need to cope – just like the airline instructions, *"Place the oxygen mask over your own mouth first and then assist your children with theirs."*

If parents are quarreling and fighting, they need to seek guidance for their marriage. Going through a crisis is hard enough but even more so when you aren't getting along. Children watch and are affected by the marital conflict. If the parents aren't operating as a team, they need to "fix" the team.

**Talking to children about a farm or ranch crisis.** During hard times, parents need to get away from their own troubles and spend more time listening to their children. First listen, then talk. Ask, "What's life like on a farm (or ranch)?" Or better yet, ask, "What's life like on *this* farm (or ranch)?" See how they respond. Children need an opportunity to express their fears and worries about what they see and feel.

If you hear something that bothers you, stay in the listening mode and draw them out completely before responding to their concerns. Besides your own example of coping responsibly yourself, being a caring listener is the biggest help you can give.

Next, be honest in describing the financial implications of the crisis for the family. Rand Conger says "brutally honest." Keep them appraised of the decisions and plans you have for dealing with it. Explain your moods, edginess, preoccupation and apologize for any unfairness due to your own stress reactions. Children can handle material losses OK if their family relationships are solid. By sharing your financial struggles with them, you enlist their active support, cooperation and contributions to the family's well being.

Young people whose hearts were set on "taking over" someday need to verbalize their concerns about their dreams being in jeopardy. Oftentimes youth are more flexible in changing career focus and adapt well. It is the parents who need to figure out what is best for themselves and not carry undo guilt about what may or may not happen in their children's future careers.

**How schools and churches can help.** As friends of rural children, caring adults can be aware and listen to them about their worries and concerns. Seek out and engage them by asking about their lives.

The farm crisis and its impact can be a topic of discussion in classrooms. This will normalize the problem for rural children suffering through it. Videotaped stories about the crisis or workbooks may also spur discussion. Schools can be mindful of expenses connected with extra-curricular activities. Also, church and community events recognizing the plight of farm families will help reduce the isolation rural children feel.

# How Children Learn To Bounce Back

In 1989, Dr. Werner, a University of Chicago sociologist, reported on 31 years of observation of children growing up in chronic poverty, highlighting the qualities of survivors of dysfunctional families and neighborhoods. He found that one out of three high risk children grew into competent young adults who loved well, worked well and played well. He describes this skill among survivor children as resiliency.

**Resilient.** Don't you love that word, resilient? It is one of the words in the English language that gives a feel for its meaning just in the way it trips off the tongue. There is a bounce in the word as in the actions it represents.

Resilient: the ability to bounce back after being pressed; recovering in strength, humor and spirit after difficulty.

According to Werner, " None [of the 1/3] developed serious learning or behavior problems in childhood or adolescence. ..they succeeded in school, managed home and social life well and set realistic educational and vocational goals and expectations for themselves... We found a number of protective factors [describing 'survivor' children] in the families, outside of the family circle and within the resilient children themselves that enabled them to resist stress."

Werner felt the children tended to "...be sociable, be active, be affectionate, be easygoing, be highly active yet not distressed, try new experiences and ask for help when needed. As the child got older, he or she became particularly adept at recruiting attention from 'surrogate parents' when biological parents were not available."

**What do resilient people do?** They:
* have an active approach toward solving life's problems
* perceive their experiences constructively
* have an ability to gain others' positive attention
* have an ability to maintain a positive vision of a
  meaningful life
Resiliency isn't just about coping; it is about excelling. Other

studies by Bloom and Csikszentmihalyi have shown these same processes are responsible for the development of great talent or outstanding performance - a formula for success.

Psychologists Dennis Embry, Valerie Rauluk and Michael Krupnick of Heartsprings Inc. in Tucson, AZ have expanded the definition of resiliency to include the following:

* **Inner meaning** - Being aware of and developing significance inside of yourself that provides for intrinsic learning and motivation.

* **Self-regulation** - Controlling your approach to learning by thinking about how you are thinking...

* **Feeling of competence** - Knowing you have the ability to do a particular thing. Lack of this tool results in laziness and other avoidance behaviors; presence of this tool often results in feeling confident and motivated to learn.

* **Goal directed behavior** - Taking initiative in setting, seeking, and reaching objectives on a consistent basis.

* **Self-development** - Being aware of your uniqueness as an individual and working toward becoming all you can be.

* **Sharing behavior** - Communicating thoughts to yourself and others in a manner that make underlying assumptions known.

* **Feeling of challenge** - Being aware of the effects emotions have on novel, complex and consequently difficult tasks; knowing how to deal with challenge.

* **Awareness of self-change** - Knowing that change happens throughout life and learning to expect, nurture and benefit from it.

That is a remarkable list of qualities that a child from a high risk environment obtains by his or her ability to seek and enlist the aid of at least one functional parent, relative or caring adult mentor. This experience with a meaningful adult provides guidance, excitement, attention, encouragement, and a model for coping with challenges. The child feels valued and loved.

Children from all backgrounds can benefit from exposure to caring adults that intersect their lives in some way. It is people like teachers, coaches, church youth leaders, Scout and 4-H volunteers, Big Brothers/Big Sisters and 'grandparent' volunteers in the classroom that cross generational boundaries to provide a motivational force in a child's life.

Youths themselves need to learn give service and take social responsibility for others through involvement with projects and groups that are doing good. - with a generous dose of adult guidance and contact.

We are an age-segregated society. These cross-generational contacts used to happen naturally within the context of small town living and readily available grandparents and relatives. Now the grandparents live far away and the children's lives are peer dominated. Positive peer relationships can provide a boost but do not substitute for the skill fundamental to childhood resiliency - recruiting adult attention.

Resilient - the ability to bounce back after being pressed; recovering in strength, humor and spirit after difficulty. Life certainly has its difficulties and losses. What we need is resilience.

# Youth Asks Questions About Farm Crisis

In April 2000, I received some questions from a young woman who wrote for her high school newspaper in Bismarck, North Dakota. Here are her questions and my answers.

**What kind of emotional toll can operating a struggling family farm have on a family, in particular the children of the family?**

The parents are subject to incredible money pressures in trying to pay off farm loans and other farm related bills along with meeting family living expenses. They also face the prospect of not getting loans renewed for the coming farming year and are worrying about their ability to farm. This represents a threat to a way of life they cherish and causes emotional turmoil, apprehension, depression, fear, despair, escapist and avoidance coping, irritability, sleep problems, anger and blame and marriage conflict.

Some of the chief ways children are affected is through their worry about parental conflict, being recipients of a conflict that spills over into parent/child relationships, and parental depression. Depression takes a toll on parent/child relationships because Mom and Dad aren't emotionally available to be able to tune into their children's lives. They can't monitor their children's activities the way they should. Some teens, particularly young men, may have their hearts set on farming and are apprehensive - just like their parents - about their own future in farming.

**How can the family - in particular the young - deal with the problems involved in a struggling family farm? How can they cope?**

They can cope by talking with each other and supporting one another. They can analyze their financial position, communicate with their lender, examine options either in or out of farming, and get as much advice or information about their situation as possible. It helps to find others to confide in regarding either their emotional struggle or their financial situation. They also need to be sharing the family's dilemma with their children so they can understand the emotions and distractions whirling around in the family.

Teens need to be as supportive and as helpful as possible. Good memories can come from a crisis like this if children can pitch in and offer support to their parents. Children can ask hard questions and get Mom and Dad to share their thoughts. Children can consciously remove any guilt or pressure by letting their parents know they don't need to farm for their sake.

Above all, they don't need to be adding additional stress and worry by causing conflict or disobeying family rules and values. If there is anything farm families love more than a farming lifestyle, it is their children. They don't need additional discipline problems.

**What should a teen wishing to take over the family farm**

**know and expect before getting into it?**

Farming is a stressful profession subject to many forces outside of one's personal control. It is extremely competitive. The work commitments are longer than others make in society. The asset base of the family farm should be sufficient to support the families who chose to farm, provide for the parent's retirement and be capable of surviving "down" years in farming. Teens need to know the basic trends in agriculture: technology, marketing, global economy and getting bigger versus specialty crops. They need to be comfortable with a business orientation to farming.

They also need to get as much training and education as possible before coming back to the farm so that they have options for supplementing farm income through auxiliary businesses and off-farm work. They need to size-up their parent's willingness to share decisions in a democratic way so that they, as adult children, can have influence over their own futures.

**With crop prices at rock bottom and equipment prices shooting through the roof, is there any prospect for a successful future in family farming? Is there anything to keep their spirits up?**

Basic optimism is essential to farming. Farming runs in cycles and the good years have been a part of survival. The advent of computer technology, the global economy and communications means fewer windfall profits in the future. But there are also opportunities for niche marketing. Value-added products and cooperative arrangements among farmers offer clout in the marketplace.

Population growth and improving economies in certain countries in the developing world will lead to an increase in the quality of their diets. This will mean opportunities for continued export markets for farm products. The farm has to be competitive in this new economy and will have to be adept in finding and maintaining markets.

**What misconceptions are there about family farms? What should teens like myself, who are not particularly involved in**

**farming, know about family farms?**

The biggest misconception is that life on the farm is peaceful and stress-free. It is complicated, stressful and extremely competitive. It is rewarding, but the family farm lifestyle comes with a price. It is difficult to make profits in a mature, highly competitive industry where one can do everything right and still fail due to the weather, lack of control over prices, international trade, government regulation and politics.

**Should the terrible shape of family farms these days distress the public?**

There are many families hurting and who need assistance through programs that help them transition off the farm. The government and public need to support programs to help these families make good transitions. It is a humane and compassionate response to the changes in the farm economy.

In the larger picture, the reduction of family farmers may eventually result in higher food prices to the consumer. From an environmental standpoint, nobody cares for the land like family farmers who are committed to long range productivity of their own land.

**Does the ethnic background of North Dakota have anything to do with how farming difficulties are handled?**

Germanic and Scandinavian farmers have family farming as a part of their heritage. As such, the commitment to farming is more tenacious and persistent and consequently the emotional fallout is greater when the farm fails. Their formula for success becomes a formula for pain when farming is no longer possible. They may be in denial longer and not be emotionally prepared to leave farming. There are feelings of failing both the past and future generations by their decision to quit.

# Making Holiday Traditions
# On A Low Budget

During a down year farm families may need to tighten their belts and make do during the holiday season. It isn't easy to pinch pennies when the rest of society seems to be rolling along. Also, going through the uncertainty and worry about the farm economy detracts from a festive mood.

The best way to avoid getting caught in the intense demand of the holiday is to keep your celebration simple. Figure out what makes the holidays meaningful to your family and let go of the extras that don't make the list. Once people identify what is truly important, then they can enjoy the season instead of feeling pushed by obligations.

Here are a few examples of what should be family priorities.

**Use the holidays to teach and celebrate.** Use the occasion to teach important family values and religious traditions. For most of us, the religious significance of the birth of Jesus Christ gives meaning to our lives. The holiday encompasses people from other faiths and secular persuasions as well.

The holidays are a time for renewal of faith and charity. It is a season of love, and giving love will help get farm families away from their troubles. By its traditions, a family shows that it cares about certain things deeply. Christmas traditions are a way to define who you are, what you believe and how special you are to each other.

Holiday decorations and heirlooms that come down through the family have special stories behind them. As you decorate, talk about the memories behind the holiday keepsakes.

**Family togetherness**. The holidays are about loving ties with family and friends. These relationships give you a chance to make the extra effort in finding ways to share that love.

The travel, expense and sacrifice of family and friends to get together during the holiday season are worth the effort. This is a wonderful time to put your arms around one another and cherish these moments together. Openly share your worries and troubles, and you'll invite people to express their care for you.

If possible, involve your children with their grandparents. Grandparents offer different information and perspective than any other relationship. They act as carriers of the family tradition. They link the grandchildren to the past and help them understand their place in the ongoing saga of the family.

**Gift-giving.** Families on limited incomes can create financial problems for themselves and add unwanted stress by overextending themselves. Overspending at Christmas can take away from other living expenses for months to come. Buying on credit shows up in interest payments, sometimes for months to come.

Whatever your income, determine how much money you can afford to spend on gifts. Talk to family members and let them know there is less money available for giving. Shift the emphasis on family fun and experiences together instead of on gifts.

When it comes to gift-giving, it is the thought and not the expense that counts. Gift giving shouldn't be a burden and take the joy out of the occasion.

Memorable Christmases happen when people are forced to use their ingenuity and creativity to "make do" with personal, well-thought-out gifts. Examples might include something handcrafted or a gift certificate of time or talent. One or two special but simple gifts can create a wonderful memory or bond.

**The gift of time.** Time is more precious than money. When there is no money, you can still give of your time and talents. Enjoy some special one-to-one time with your children or grandchildren during the holiday. Each relationship is different. Give of yourself completely with the one you are with. Make sure each child goes away thinking he or she is special, because they are!

Go on outings. Read to them. Talk to them. Listen to them. Play cards or board games. Build puzzles. Have family fun and make memories.

Teach them something *only* you can teach them. Share your

talents and work together on one of your projects - Swedish bread, special cookies, building a model or whatever you do that is special.

Another gift could be stories from your past that connect them with their roots. Tell them stories about your memories of your past, stories from your past holidays.

**Reaching out to others.** There is a simple formula for those who find themselves in unfortunate situations. Find someone less fortunate than yourself and lift his or her spirit. It's true. When you lift another's burden, your own will be lighter. *Give even if you don't have much to give.* You can give of yourself and that is a lot to give.

Make a visit. Remember the lonely and the infirm. Make a phone call. Send an e-mail. Write a letter. Give a meal invitation. Recognize a loss. Listen to a sad heart. Your open heart is needed by a world with too much loneliness and suffering in it.

Better yet, for the best kind of holiday memory, involve your children in a family activity of helping someone else. Help your children learn to give. Help them put thought and their own money into their gift giving. They will discover the special joy that comes from giving and be less concerned about receiving.

Take a challenge to make this your best Christmas ever. Remember the reason for the season!

*CHAPTER FIVE*

# DEALING WITH DEBT

## Is Family Farming That Special?

I presented a videotape of a farm family discussing their exit from agriculture to a conference of plant scientists. On the tape, an 18 year-old son mentioned he was going to study agronomy in college and choose a profession close to farming. His father expressed his guilt that none of his sons would be able to farm. The mother, obviously emotionally hurt by farming and the farm crisis, expressed her relief that her sons wouldn't have to farm even though she would have preferred that they would have had that choice for themselves.

During my remarks I commented that in the audience were probably some that chose to be plant scientists for similar reasons. Sure enough, after my talk a few people did come up and tell me how they had come from farm backgrounds and made their career choice after it became obvious that they couldn't farm.

**Parents haven't failed.** Another speaker on the program, agricultural economist Steven Sonka from the University of Illinois, took exception to some of my remarks and we had a spirited discussion after the program. The gist of what he said was that in no other profession do parents feel like failures if their children don't succeed them in their profession. He feels there are lots of honorable professions and careers and lots of ways to be happy in life. His children won't go through life feeling like failures if they don't turn out to be college professors or have a "Ph.D." after their name.

Dr. Sonka felt that reinforcing the message that farmers have a way of life so superior to the rest of society is a wrong message – a disservice and an unfair burden. It leads to deep disappointment and hurt for either the parents or to the children if one of them doesn't succeed the parents on the farm.

I shared with Dr. Sonka my concern that ex-farmers or farmers contemplating leaving agriculture need to learn that there is a good life waiting for them – that they are good, talented and can be happy doing other work. They need to understand that living in a city or a town has its advantages and isn't the "bugaboo" they always thought it would be. They also need to learn that it is possible to raise healthy, happy children in the city and life on a family farm isn't the only way to turn out good kids.

**Emotional baggage.** Though not everything could be said during that brief conversation, it got me to thinking. In my counseling career, I've seen plenty of emotional baggage connected with keeping the farm in the family:

- Children who feel pressured and guilty if they don't go into farming and carry on the family legacy of keeping the farm in the family.
- Parents who would like to quit farming feeling pressured to stay on by a child whose heart is set on being a farmer.
- Middle-aged farmers who have become disillusioned with farming but feel trapped by family expectations.
- Farmers who always wanted to try another profession but feel trapped by family expectations.
- Highly successful parents in retirement years feeling like failures because their children chose not to farm.
- A few farmers who chose suicide because they didn't measure up to goals that became impossible.

I've also seen parents who are open-minded and consciously

encourage their children to try other fields. But their kids aren't so open-minded. They have a love affair going with the farm already and they can't wait to farm. Where does that motivation come from if it doesn't come from the parents?

It comes from children who like growing up on a farm. They enjoy teamwork and the responsibility of being a part of the farm. They like the feeling of competence they've gained from learning multiple farming skills and know-how. They enjoy the closeness to nature and animals.

They enjoy the togetherness of family life on a farm. Many have positive experiences working with their fathers. They observe a farm marriage bringing happiness to both their parents. They enjoy the friendships and closeness of a rural community. The motivation comes from wanting to raise their children on a family farm.

**Family farming has changed.** But family farming as a way of life or as a place to raise children is on the way out. Farming is big business. Modern farming is about rapidly advancing technology, expensive land and equipment, huge financial investments and risks, marketing, the lack of control over the weather, prices and high stress.

The farming life the children fell in love with and family farming in the future may be two different things. Children need to let go of their illusions and expectations of what farming should or used to be and instead pay attention to what it is actually turning out to be.

Parents don't need the crushing legacy of feeling successful only if the farm is kept in the family. It is wonderful if it can happen – when there is a viable opportunity and a willing child who is making their own choice to farm. Children don't need to carry the burden of parents' dreams as their own. They need to find and live their own dream.

Keeping the farm in the family or family farming can be wonderful goals. These twin goals can also be a two-edged sword that cuts both ways if they cannot be realized. Family farming is special but not that special.

# Four Flaws That Get Farmers Into Trouble

I visited with a lender about four common weaknesses he sees farmers have in their management. Here are some of his ideas about farmers who still fall short in their management.

**1. Marketing.** In the past, farmers may have been burned by a bad experience with hedges and options in the futures market. Futures are still the way to go. Farmers need to lock in their prices to maximize their returns. The markets are too volatile to do it any other way.

This lender believes that a lack of reliance on futures marketing reflects a problem with pride. Many available marketing seminars are poorly attended. This is also true for programs on records, taxes, and risk management/insurance.

Why? He believes operators, no matter whether they are big or small, are afraid to be seen there. It is an ego thing. If they do attend, some of the concepts go over their head. They don't want to appear stupid in front of their peers so they don't ask enough questions. They leave and market the same old way they always have.

What is that same old way? The gambler and speculator in them wants to hit the market at its peak so they hold the crop too long and incur interest and storage costs. This is an ego thing also. There are bragging rights to selling at just the right time. This lender feels the maturity date of loans is a major factor in marketing or else even more farmers would hold on to their crops too long.

He also feels believes that women aren't as attached to commodities or as ego involved as their husbands and consequently make better marketers. They take the emotion out of it and can make more dispassionate decisions.

Women may be more security conscious and more aware of cash flow needs for family living. They see the need to lock in a price. One gift he sees farm women bringing to farm management is their orientation for detail. Also they are willing to go to seminars and ask the "dumb" questions.

He would like to see farmers execute a marketing plan - any plan. He guesses that only 15 percent of the farmers he knows are really where they need to be when it comes to marketing.

**2. Using records for management.** This isn't about the days when farmers ran their businesses out of shoe boxes stuffed with receipts. Most farmers have computerized their records and have accurate, accessible information. Their accountants have good information.

This lender thinks that farmers don't know what the records mean. They need to learn how to evaluate their records in order to make better business decisions. Farmers can use key ratios and indicators as tools for management decisions. Only a small percentage of farmers actively use their records as a key part of their management. The problem is similar to the marketing issue - the pride factor of not being willing to ask questions.

**3. Family living expenses.** This is a delicate area. A lot of farmers are still farming because they have cut their family living to the bone. They feel the pain of working hard and not having enough income to pay the bills. There is real hurt and hardship in the countryside.

This is about farm families who don't keep track of family living expenses. They write checks without knowing where they stand. During hard times, their lifestyle doesn't change. They live like a family whose living expenses are independent of farm income.

They still trade pickups and take extravagant vacations. "We work hard. We owe it to ourselves." Instead of cutting back, they add debt to an already precarious financial situation. The lender sees too much credit card debt coming in to maintain their lifestyle when they should be in a cut back mode.

**4. Communicating with others.** During a time of crisis, farmers tend to keep their own counsel and try to solve problems without gathering enough advice or consultation. They need to be active in their communications with their lenders/creditors and be honest and forthright about their difficulties. They hide from bad news and don't want to face reality.

By withdrawing and keeping their problems to themselves, they either become depressed or immobilized. They can become angry and scapegoat their problems on others. The solutions lie in facing reality, communicating with others and being flexible. Problems can be solved if they overcome their fear of exposing their problems to others.

# Ag Financial Counselors Advice: Start Early, Get Help

I was invited to participate in a training program with the South Dakota Ag Mediation and Financial Counselors. I also consulted with Willard Brunelle, an ag financial consultant, who serves northwestern Minnesota.

The Ag Finance Counselors shared with me their observations on some of the self-defeating behavior they observe when they meet with clients. They also shared their ideas on what farmers could do differently to avoid the depth of financial and emotional pain that accompanies financial crisis.

1. **Seek out professional health resources for depression and suicidal thinking.** Medication and counseling together are extremely important in treating depression. Physical ailments are one way the stress and depression are manifest. Seek out family physicians, clergy, outreach workers, and the extension service for ideas on where to go for assistance.

2. **Keep the faith.** Look to a higher power. Keep attending your church. Find support in a spiritual setting or in a support group. Hold your head up and let your friends know what is really going on with you. Social withdrawal and shame turn the problems inward, exactly where they don't need to go. Move into the future in a proactive sense. Don't dwell on mistakes. Don't blame your-

self for things you had no control over.

3. **Keep the family together.** When a farm gets close to not having enough assets to keep farming, there is almost always marital discord. Decisions to continue to dump income into the farm causes conflict, especially when it is the wife's off-farm income which is barely keeping the farming operation afloat at the expense of family living and high stress.

Couples need to be mutually supportive and work through their solutions together instead of withdrawing into isolated, aggressive or lonely positions. Ag counselors often find that by the time they arrive at a farmstead they have two clients with two opposing agendas.

Marital tension needs to be addressed quickly through outside guidance. Get a good word-of-mouth referral on who can help you. Ag financial counselors believe that many times divorce could have been headed off if the couple had started two years sooner. They estimate that discipline problems with teen-agers begin about 18 months after a financial crisis begins.

Pride is a factor. Farmers want to put up a good front with their local clergy and professionals. They don't really turn a corner and get the help they need until they stop worrying about what others think. They also need to be assured of confidentiality.

4. **Start sooner to get help.** Don't try to work through the process alone. Farmers in this position need help with decision-making and information about tax and legal consequences. Ideally, it takes one to three years to dissolve a farming operation while slowly winding down.

Be careful to select accountants and attorneys who have a good understanding of "farm law." Too many farmers rely on "hearsay" or gossip in the farm community about how to solve their problems without actually turning to other experts for a second or third opinion.

The financial counselors agreed that most of the time they are getting to these farmers about one to two years too late to prevent the financial wrecks they find when they first make contact. Too many families are not realistic when it comes to their family living expenses. They guess too low. They live on credit cards. If the bank cuts them off, they turn to their credit cards as a quick fix.

One ag financial counselor felt that what is needed is a "wellness" model. The financial ideas and help they offer could help salvage farmers' equity if the process were started soon enough.

**5. Make tough family decisions.** Trying to farm together (father and son operations) may jeopardize the financial viability of both operations. The son may have a better shot at financing or face the reality of not being able to farm without the parents' involvement. Perhaps both families are too unrealistic in their approach to farming. Too many people are trying to earn a living on too few acres.

Big mistakes are made when the parents go out on a limb to keep their children in farming and end up losing their own farm. Farmers may ignore reality in order to keep a son or a son-in-law in farming. These kinds of decisions are best made with outside consulting to take the emotion out of the decision-making process and to wrestle with what the numbers actually mean.

**6. Don't wait until the last minute.** Don't put off paperwork to the bank until the last minute. Farmers may end up getting the bank decision about the status of their operational loans too close to spring planting. By then they have made decisions and commitments so, if they are denied their loan, they try to farm with main street credit and credit cards.

Interest rates are atrocious and their finances continue to spiral downward. There are other ways of financing that are shaky if not shady. Be careful of other financing schemes. Main street and credit card debt adds to the family's woes and problems.

Late filers are often so busy with day-to-day operations that they ignore the future and long term planning. The later they file their loan applications and financial statements, the greater the likelihood that they haven't discussed their plans with anyone and haven't rehearsed their answers or presentation. By preparing early, they have a chance to get some input from an advisor before trying to "sell" the bank.

Late filers too often may be hoping for outside help like government bailouts or deadline extensions. Putting off decisions or reviewing their finances is a way of continuing to deny their problems.

I have nothing but admiration for ag financial counselors. They are truly on the front lines for mental health, family well being, and financial concerns. They listen. They don't judge. They develop trust. They care. They are wise. They are patient. They make good referrals. They like their opportunities to help farm families in trouble. The main thing they wish is that they could be on the scene a lot sooner to prevent some of the pain and suffering their clients experience.

# Farmers And Lenders: Yikes! Now What Do We Do?

Most farmers and ranchers have operating loans to handle the production year. The lender and ag borrower work together to project goals, profits, cash flows and capital requirements for the year.

With agriculture, both parties are taking a risk. Sometimes, normal assumptions made when the loan was drawn up may not hold up.

So now what happens to the farmer/lender relationship? How can lenders and ag borrowers work as a team to resolve difficulties about repayment and recovery? Here are some ideas.

**What the lender wants:**

**Be open and honest.** The lender wants a fair shot at helping the distressed producer deal with any problems. Problems aren't going to go away by themselves. With good communications, they can give each other a chance to make adjustments. The sooner everyone knows, the better the results.

Feeling anxious and scared about the lender's reactions to the disaster is natural. Ag lenders are usually a caring bunch. They have farm backgrounds and are highly sympathetic to farmers. They will offer support, ideas and hard work to get through a tough time.

If you hide problems or go around the lender's back to take on new debt you'll break down the trust you need with your primary source of credit. Being honest when things are going good is easier than when times are bad. Don't let your lender hear about your problems or financial dealings on the street.

**Walk the talk.** Behavior is predictable by what farmers do, not by the lip service they give to their goals. Don't tell your lender what he or she wants to hear and then go and do as you please anyway. Follow the plan you've set out. If you do, you'll receive trust when you need it the most.

**Be realistic.** Be willing to shoot for reasonable and obtainable goals. Borrowers who are caught up in dreams kid themselves and adopt "pie in the sky" projections. The biggest dreamers are farmers who feel "entitled" to farm and see farming as a way of life instead of a business.

It is the common sense producer who deals with problems straight on that wins the confidence of the lender. Farmers should know their cost of production, breakeven points and be realistic about projected income. The financial management of the business is as important as the production side.

Lenders appreciate producers who have a healthy respect for debt. Lenders like to see someone who is willing to cut back rather than expand their way out of trouble. Borrowers who don't have self-discipline with their lifestyle or run up credit card debt usually aren't good at controlling their operating costs. The answer to a problem isn't always a bigger loan.

**What the borrower wants:**

**Respect the hard work, dignity and pride involved in agriculture.** If personalities clash, change a loan officer to someone the farmer can work with. Problems can be solved with time, effort and the right people. Give the farmer time to come up with the right answers instead of imposing them on him. Sometimes it takes time for emotions to settle.

If partial liquidations or other workout situations occur, assume some of the losses. Leave a little something on the table so farmers can have a fair chance of holding their heads high and rebuilding their lives. The respect you show distressed borrowers when they are feeling bad means a great deal.

Take your customers as they are. Some farmers aren't as financially astute as others or as you'd like them to be. Be patient and take the time to let them know what you expect. Many of your clients may not be perfect customers but they are still bankable.

**Keep it professional.** Live up to your agreements. Inform producers right away if there is a problem. Don't hold back bad news. Give them time to correct the problem. Insults, blame and anger are part of an emotional response to stress. Don't take it personally and overreact to expressions of raw emotion.

Don't take over problems or micro-manage decisions. Farmers can live with the results when consequences come from their own decisions. The roles of the lender making credit decisions and farmers making farming decisions and living with the outcome need to be clear.

As strange as it seems, if a lender has been too friendly and close to the family, it may be embarrassing to approach the bank during a crisis. Perhaps a switch to another loan officer can ease the way to more honest and frank conversations.

# Getting Along With Your Lender

It is a delicate time when the farmer or rancher sits down with a lender and projects income, expenses and profitability. What can you do to make this relationship work best?

**1. Remember, this is a partnership.** It is a key relationship outside of the family arena that is essential for business success. It is in the lender's best interest to have the loan repaid on time and that there are profits for the producer. That is the goal. You are both working for the same thing.

**2. Include your spouse.** Women need to be included in these discussions so they know where they stand with debt and the status of the farm in terms of equity and income projections. Women who aren't included aren't informed and can't serve as sounding boards or provide that needed reality check.

Farming and ranching are hard, stressful professions. It is the emotional and family support that gets people through the tough times. Your lender will have more confidence in your operation if he or she sees the two of you working together and equally familiar with the stakes and obligations of the coming year.

**3. Be good at communicating.** Take every opportunity to communicate in a positive, proactive manner. Your lender should hear about your problems directly from you. Be quick to communicate openly about your situation. Almost all lenders are interested, caring people who want to solve problems if they are given a chance early on to work with you. You don't win points by staying away - even if there are some fears and unknowns with the situation.

**4. Be honest.** Trust is the cornerstone of all good relationships. Don't violate your trust succumbing to the pressures of finance. Don't rationalize your values in order to justify a deceptive or illegal action. No matter what happens, keep your integrity. Your straight forward dealings will stand you in good stead with your lender as in life.

**5. Watch your emotions.** There are so many factors outside of a farmer's control that it is easy to feel angry, upset and frustrated. Life isn't fair. The hard work of farming and ranching isn't always rewarded. The markets and the weather mess up the best plans.

It harms the lender/borrower relationship to blame and take out your frustrations with the most visible player in an economy that goes haywire from time to time. Your lending institution is trying to survive in that same environment. To clash and shut off communications by angry outbursts doesn't help. The feeling tone of the negotiations should be friendly, courteous, respectful and pleasant, even if hard things are talked about.

**6. Be good at negotiating.** Good negotiators radiate confidence in their ideas. They have an appreciation for the key limits or needs on the other side of the desk.

Find out about the lender's concerns. Have a working knowledge of what those factors are and show by your plan how you want to satisfy their basic requirements. The best negotiators know the other fellow's concerns almost as well as their own.

Don't just dump a problem and expect the other partner to solve it. Come in with your plans, know your numbers and what they mean. Show how you expect to repay the loan. Projections have to be realistic given the state of supplies and the weak export market.

One common expectation of lenders is that you come in with a marketing plan. Almost any plan will do. Have something in place that shows you know when you are going to sell your production, at what levels and what the profits might be. Holding on to crops or livestock to hit market peaks is too risky in today's volatile farm economy.

Be conversant with your family living budget and how you are living with that plan. Lack of discipline about personal record keeping and decision-making creates doubt about your overall management of the operating loan. This is one area of concern for lenders who see credit card debt and big purchases during a down year. These are red flags of poor fiscal management.

agement of the operating loan. This is one area of concern for lend-ers who see credit card debt and big purchases during a down year. These are red flags of poor fiscal management.

**7. Find someone who believes in you.** Not everybody hits it off right. Personality clashes can get in the way of business. If for some reason you don't hit it off with a particular lender, don't be afraid to ask for a change. It is the relationship that makes this work. The lending institution sees it the same way. They want open and respectful communication.

If communications have broken down, get an outside media-tor to come with you to help get communications rolling. A third party can help spot problems and make helpful suggestions.

# Breaking Through Denial During Hard Times

The thing that farmers and ranchers do best is trouble shoot-ing and problem-solving. With the day-to-day challenges of produc-tion agriculture, a farmer or rancher has no equal. It is when they have to deal with the gloomy reality of markets, high operating ex-penses, and rapidly escalating debt that they may be paralyzed into inaction.

The commitments, goals and emotions that underpin rural life run deep. Emotion interferes with rational thinking. The situa-tion may call for radical changes, changes that one does not want to make. Usually the unwillingness to deal with reality is on the side of the family where the land has been passed on from previous genera-tions. Most of the time it is on the male side of the family.

So what do you do if you are a farm or ranch woman and your husband can't bring himself to deal with the real problems?

- **Talk over the big picture as you understand it.** If there is some key information you don't have, ask about it and insist on getting to the facts. Let him know that you expect his re-action to what you have said. Give him a couple of days to mull it over and then approach the subject again.

• **Use good listening techniques.** Don't try to solve problems in anger. Both of you need to understand each other's percep-tions and judgments of reality, and communicate that under-standing. Be quietly persistent in dealing with the topic, not in an angry or forceful manner.

If you, as a couple, have difficulty communicating - being angry, bringing up the past, changing the subject, interrupt-ing, walking off, not getting through, criticizing, blaming, etc. - you may need a third party to help you gain skills be-fore you can solve problems together. Here the financial cri-sis has highlighted a problem that perhaps needed addressing all along.

• **Know where you stand.** Get the books and financial records in order. There is nothing like facts and figures as a dose of cold reality. Let your husband explain his best scenario of meeting the debt crisis. Based on what you know, give him your idea of what the options might be. From your perspec-tive, let him know what decisions need to be made right away. Get his reaction. If he objects, ask him to explain what will or won't work from his point of view. If you have gotten him this far, you've opened up a dialogue.

• **Ask for a financial consultant.** You need a second opinion of your status and options. Sometimes the opinion of the lend-ing agency is distrusted and having another opinion makes the problem real. There are many financial advisors and me-diators that may be contacted through the state department of agriculture. Projections can be worked out for basic enter-prises for the coming year. Your consultant will have ideas on what options you might have to restructure, defer or me-diate the debt.

The consultant will gently help him realize if his plan will or will not pencil out. If your husband's plan is based on "blue sky" assumptions, someone else will be asking the hard questions and not you. If his plan has a chance, maybe you'll be the one that will find renewed hope.

- **Agree to disagree.** If you have the wherewithal to go another year, establish a time line in which you both agree to work on his plan. At the end of that time you can sit down with the new facts and figures and decide what comes next. By then perhaps he may be able to see if all his hard work and anxiety has made a dent in the problem.

- **Get help.** If your husband is depressed, suggest a visit with a professional - a family doctor, minister, good friend - someone that will help him express his feelings and get further help. A depressed person often can't make good decisions until their depression has been lifted. If your suggestions fail, insist on getting help and make the arrangements. Part of the problem with depression is that the depressed person has become immobilized and needs someone to take charge.

- **Be honest about your feelings.** If your not happy with the farm or ranch lifestyle and finances, explain carefully about what you need. If you, your marriage or your family is suffering, explain why. Your happiness counts and he needs to figure you into the solution.

- **Talk over your basic goals.** The farm and ranch is a means to an end, not an end in itself. Someone is going to have to sacrifice. If you have goals in common, you can work together, support each other, talk and solve problems. When your goals are different, you'll be pulling against one another, no matter how loving or skilled your communication might be.

Leaving the farm or ranch is a huge decision that may take more than a year to make. Start the dialogue early so that no matter what you do, you can go through the crisis together. Express confidence in him and his abilities. Help him dust himself off and get going again.

There are four things couples need to make it through a financial crisis: love, faith, flexibility and communications. Someday you'll look back and be grateful for those days when you pulled together as a couple. It will strengthen your bond.

# Avoid Foreclosure At All Costs

*I received a story from a farmer who was forced out of agriculture in 1998. He had many insights about the emotional and legal aspects of his battle with his lending institution. He titles his unpublished manuscript, "Final Harvest." (The following quotations are excerpts from Chapter Five "Don't do it and why not.")*

I doubt that any of you has ever read and studied every word in that pile of papers you were asked to sign when you closed a loan. I assure you they give your lender every single advantage fine legal minds tempered with years operational experience could possibly put on paper. Somewhere on those pages they make sure that if all payments are not made, YOU will have the honor of paying all collection costs.

If you were a relatively naive farm boy like me who never dreamed he would ever miss a payment, you probably easily agreed to your lenders seemingly endless quest for collateral and when you left his building that closing day, he had in his possession what amounted to a blank check on your net worth.

... When you break the provisions of your loan contract and your loan meets the criteria, when it crosses some defined line, you cease being a customer and are seemingly transformed into, for lack of a better word, the enemy. In all fairness to the institution, when the transformation occurs, various state laws that were passed to protect the debtor, are activated.

The state laws generally assume there is an adversarial relationship between lender and debtor and strict procedures must be followed or the lender may lose the right to collect. There will be no friendly chat with your loan officer any more. In fact he will probably lead you to another part of the building and introduce you to the person that will, "be your contact in the future."

... Whether you know it or not you are now paying a very expensive lawyer to plot your own demise. Your lender almost certainly has used one of those blank checks against your net worth to buy very expensive legal advice even though their own "collector" has knowledge and experience that far exceeds yours.

Hopefully you will now again feel my spirit reach out from this page, throw you up against the wall and lovingly slap your face a couple of times to make sure I have your undivided attention for what I am now going to say. If you have not yet searched out and hired the very best bankruptcy attorney you can find, YOU MUST DO IT NOW. [Later in the chapter, the author suggests even better advice, "You should never let the foreclosure begin."]

...Well, if there ever was a time for you to be a realist, it is now. You are in a war. Your opponent has knowledge, experience and, a very expensive lawyer you are paying for that is leading the attack. They know the laws, the tactics and where you are vulnerable. It would be insane not to have someone on your side that knows your rights under the law and the tactics used in this kind of war. Someone smart and knowledgeable who is not emotionally involved that can keep you in touch with reality.

... I often used to wonder why lenders never wanted to lend more than sixty or at the most, seventy percent of market value on such stable assets as land. There is almost always some inflation which should make land worth more each year, at least monetarily. And each year you make payments, the land has greater collateral value to the lender.

... There are a lot of factors that affect the sale of an asset. For instance, agriculture has long term up and down cycles. I believe there is a high degree of probability that your lender's hatchet man will not agree to delay the sale of your assets a few years in order to sell at the most favorable point of the cycle. Obviously there also are better and worse times of the year to sell farm assets. Again, you should not expect your lenders AX GUY to lose any sleep worrying and working to get the prime time to sell your stuff.

Is there much of a difference between the best time of the year to sell something and the worst? You better believe it. And how about who is hired to handle the sale? I know of one potato farmer whose machinery was sold by an auctioneer who knew nothing at all about potato machinery or what it was worth. To make matters worse, the sale was held in the middle of small grain harvest. I assure you, that elderly farmer took a terrible hit that day. ...

[A couple of paragraphs from the next chapter returns to the point about delay once the legal process has started.]

... The opposition lawyer knows the institution that hired him is not paying his fees so there is no pressure for a quick settlement for him. Your own attorney probably has kids to feed too and I think it would be unfair to expect him to passionately work to end your expense, and consequently, his paycheck.

I am not necessarily suggesting that either of them is consciously or unconsciously trying to make it last, just that they have no reason to end it either - other than humanitarian. Do you see it now? You are the only person participating in the war that is crying out for it to end. The slow motion train wreck continues.

# A Loan Officer Replies

Here is a lender's response to the article about a farmer's perspective on bankruptcy and foreclosure fights.

As a 23 year Ag Loan Officer I found the article on the Successful Farmer to be vindictive and demeaning to all Ag Loan people in banks. Please allow me to give you a perspective from an Ag Loan Officer.

Our bank has never had a forced sale. We have always worked with the farmer to achieve the best result for the farmer. I am not aware of any successful farmer ever being forced to sell. Yes, we have had numerous farm sales over the years by farmers no longer able to be profitable enough to support their family and meet their financial obligations.

Our bank officers meet with their financially troubled farmers as often as necessary to work out a mutual plan. This plan does not involve an attorney, however we may request assistance of a credit counselor. Keep in mind; this plan does not happen in a day. Our discussions/counseling usually begins years before any final liquidation of the farm. The process usually goes as follows: as your author would say, "The Slow Train Wreck."

1.  Farmer and banker review a poor year; the banker makes suggestions/reviews options (maybe refinance with FSA Guarantee?) or other ideas. Then the banker states the consequences of another poor year.

2.  Farmer and banker plan next year with cautious optimism. Farmer reviews options (off farm employment?, shared farming?, letting less productive land go?, etc.). The banker emphasizes the risk and present equity position that could be jeopardized.

3.  Banker/farmer visit regularly during the year about progress and always reviews options.

**4.** Above procedure may continue for several years. However, when the banker feels the farmer is losing too much equity, he will make his recommendation. He is no longer comfortable with the progress and may recommend to sell or refinance with another lender.

**5.** Banker/farmer agree to refinance elsewhere or discontinue farming at present scale.

In this process it is most likely not, "What you say," (the lender) but, "How you say it." The lender must be honest, up-front and compassionate. These relationships are often times much more than business for us. They are personal. These are friends, not only borrowers and we have their families and best interest at heart.

We do not want to lose another family or farmer from our area, as it hurts our local community, school, businesses and, yes, the bank loses another customer. We try to make every reasonable loan possible. Loans are a major reason for a bank's existence, to serve the community and make the bank a fair profit. Banks are closely regulated by examiners to insure the loans are not of excessive risk, which would jeopardize the deposits of all of the bank's customers.

Those endless and complicated loan documents the farmers are asked to sign must have all the fine print because many prior borrowers in some parts of the country have tried to avoid paying their obligations. Some have sold mortgaged property, hid property, etc. I am not aware of loan officers asking farmers to borrow more money than is necessary for the essential farm operation.

"It's the borrower making the request and using the funds; therefore their responsibility to repay the loan." I am not saying farming is easy, however, management is a most important part. A major problem I see in farming (like anything else) is keeping up with the neighbor, new pickup, tractor, machinery, land, etc.

I was working with a young farm family for the past ten years. They had just gone through bankruptcy and were willing to start out small and work off the farm. After 10 years, I was pleased to inform the young farmer I was happy with his effort and progress. He finally had his finances under control and could weather an unforseen setback.

Guess what! Three weeks later he happily informs me he has purchased a new car, late model pickup, and tractor and has now been able to finance all the purchases elsewhere with his improved credit. Needless to say, my 10 years of counseling did not work and I do not expect this successful farmer will remain successful for long.

Some farm customers think the loan officer is some kind of robot or "AX GUY," the bank is rich and it owes them favors. The bank is a business like farming and the loan officers are human and many grew up on farms. These loan officers have stress and much responsibility that farmers do not notice. They are also compassionate and have feelings.

Like any profession, there will be a few "bad apples," but this is a free country and if the farmer does not have trust in his bank or credit institution or the loan officer, he should find another bank. I would.

Many young farmers are wanting the best of everything upfront. It's management and ambition, not the weather, that will make them successful. Of all the farmers that have left the farm in our area and have secured employment elsewhere; everyone has expressed to me that they are satisfied with their decision to leave farming. They have less stress, are happier, and see a brighter future for themselves and their family. Most say they should have left farming sooner. Who is most happy for them? I am. They are my hardworking friends.

Is there life after farming? You bet! - *Proud loan officer*

# Banking 101 And The Foreclosure Issue

*I received another hard hitting response to the column I wrote which featured a farmer's account of his foreclosure by a lending institution.*

I swear I woke up and it was 1985 when I read your article, "Avoid Foreclosure At All Costs."

Your terms, "you are in a war," "hire the very best bankruptcy attorney you can," "lender's hatchet man," "the lender's ax guy," were just great. Why didn't you fit in Posse Comitatus, American Farm Movement, FBI standoffs, PCA office and bank closings, and the lack of economic prosperity?

What's wrong with you bleeding heart liberals who think you can borrow money and never pay it back? You want capitalism without failure, which is like Christianity without hell. Why is it that the family farm espoused by politicians, radical farm groups, clinical psychologists and family business consultants should be excused from the normal course of business life and death process when a failure is experienced? I believe all the other businesses in this country are exposed to the same process without the intervention that farmers are.

Look at your points within the body of this article! "When you break the provisions of your loan contract." Why did you do this in the first place? Did you convert collateral, make unwarranted machinery and vehicle purchases or was it just the "need" for winter vacations, casinos, or keeping up with the Joneses? Why didn't you keep your lender in the circle? I've yet to see a bank that wants to close any business person out.

Believe me, it's a very unpleasant experience. I believe the truth of the matter is that you created the environment where, "there is no friendly chat." Ask yourself the question, "Where does the fault lie?"

In my 26 years of banking, I can't recall one borrower who ever paid one cent of legal fees for their own foreclosure. Obviously, you recognize and I realize that all loan documents read that way, but my experience has been that the bank has usually gone so far with the borrower that the bank does not get fees, much less interest, and in many cases a big loss of principal.

Your one-sided approach to lawyers is a dandy. My experience with bankruptcy attorneys is that their specialty is stone walling, not returning calls, not responding to written requests, hiding behind the bankruptcy court and its procedures and creating an environment of no communications. You obviously failed to recognize that time is money and money not working is a loss to a bank.

I think the truth of the matter is, most banks would get out of many of these bankruptcy deals with losses and write-offs if we could just get the borrower and their legal counsel to actively work the case. I would invite you to my town for a course in banking 101 if you think we like to put our loans on non-accrual, paying attorney's fees, charging money to loan loss reserves and using staff time for under productive hours in dealing with uncooperative, non-communicating borrowers and their lawyers. It appears to an outsider that it is strictly a loss of principal, but you don't realize that it's double and even quadruple jeopardy with the items outlined in my previous sentence.

Mr. Farmer, I went through the 1980s. I had my bank taken over by the American Farm Movement. I lived through six months of death threats called into my house during the middle of the night against me and my family and my fellow employees. I carried a pistol for a year and, by the way, with law enforcement approval. I don't want to see anything like that happen again and will leave my occupation, which I thoroughly enjoy, if it ever happens again.

When I see an article like yours promoting a general disregard for the obligations contracted with, by, and between consenting adults with no force laid on either party, I know why our country has dipped to the low point it has regarding ethics and morality. We have created an environment where no one keeps a simple contract, can tell the truth or communicate with one another from the President of the United States to professional ball players, husbands and wives and borrowers.

There are too many lawyers and too many lawyers turned politicians alone with too many clinical psychologists with pen in hand ducking anything that speaks of failure. We've pounded on the need to be successful in this country to the point that our value system has been completely abandoned. We find no good in character, honesty, truth, fair treatment, respect for others and their rights and a host of other things you fail to recognize in the body of an article you should be ashamed to have published.

In the end, I believe that your article advocated an environment that was detrimental to all aspects of society in rural America during the middle 80s. - a Minnesota banker

*I am not advocating a return to the environment of the early 80s. I believe in honesty. I believe in repaying debts. I don't want capitalism without failure. I believe in dialogue and negotiations.*

*I felt the dilemma of a farmer wanting to settle, experiencing delays and the unfairness of paying for the oppositions attorney needed to be told. Your point that you don't recall a single instance of this ever happening is reassuring. Thanks for your insight about delays and non-communication from a lender's point of view. Despite all the negativity expressed in the original column there was a statement to which you and the financially stressed farmer both agree, "You should never let foreclosure begin."*

# Should We Go Through Mediation?

What are your choices when you have a legal dispute with someone that involves a great deal of money? You go to court right?

Courtroom warriors do their best to discredit the other side and defend your side from unfair characterizations. One side is painted black and the other white. Only the facts count. The feelings get left out. Adversarial attacks leave their mark on witnesses and on their character and self-esteem.

The judge and perhaps the jury determine the outcome – in an all or nothing fashion. There is a winner and a loser. The solution is imposed. It is in the judge's hands. By going to court, you have given up control and have trust that the process will be fair. What is fair and what is legal may be two different things.

Legal proceedings cut down on room for maneuverability. It doesn't provide room for negotiating a new agreement where both sides find a way to settle their differences. If negotiations take place, they occur in an effort to avoid the risk of actually leaving the matter in the hands of the court.

Lawsuits are expensive and time consuming. It seems like they go on forever. Life is lived in limbo with the ever-present unresolved dispute casting a long shadow over your future.

Worst of all, you don't feel satisfied. You feel violated. You didn't get to say anything. There are so many feelings left unsaid. They lie there like smoldering coals or like a canker sore that was irritated but not rooted out.

**What is mediation?**

There is another way to resolve disputes short of the legal process - mediation. Mediation techniques have emerged from labor/management disputes to find widespread applications in such fields as divorce and custody issues, in public policy formation, and farmer lender disputes.

Mediation provides a process of communication to solve deadlocks. A neutral third party sets up an orderly way for disputants to talk through emotional issues and leave the actual agreements and decisions to the parties themselves. The chief concern of the mediator is to make sure that the process is fair and goes smoothly. The mediator keeps participants in line and on task.

Mediation starts with the basic assumption that people have the ability to solve their own problems. They, more than anyone, know about the problem and the range of possible solutions. With a mediator acting as a catalyst, that intimate knowledge is used to generate options or alternatives and eventually a mutually agreed upon solution.

Mediation allows people to get beyond their negative feelings and communication blocks to become creative problem-solvers in their own dispute.

The participants place confidence in the mediator to manage the conflict - to be fair to both sides and to provide a "safe" environment for the expression of feelings and concerns. The mediator tries to move the conflict into a creative problem-solving phase. The discussion on the substance of the dispute is left to the parties.

The process is confidential and records can't be subpoenaed in court. People who have been through mediation don't lose their right to go to court by entering mediation. It is a preferable step to avoid the trauma, expense and uncertainty of going to court.

The agreements are strictly voluntary. State law may mandate mediation in certain borrower/lender disputes but they do not mandate that an agreement has to be reached. Nobody is forced to enter an agreement they do not support. If people have a hand in developing an agreement, they feel better about it. They will also strive to live up to its terms better than if the terms were imposed on them.

The process is also useful if one side suspects the other of being deliberately deceptive of misleading the truth. The presence of a third party is a welcome addition. Someone else asking hard questions might smoke out the problem. It is comforting and reassuring that another person becomes aware and validates gut level feelings about what is going on. That in itself makes mediation a worthwhile process to go through.

Preparation of the financial facts and figures is similar to information needed for normal farm and ranch management and for taking the matter into court. No extra work is involved. By going to mediation farmers have nothing to lose and a whole lot to gain. Lenders who have been through this process have seen positive results and like it. Both sides have been amazed to find themselves working out a solution when they didn't feel it was possible.

**Why does mediation work?**

Left to their own devices, the disputants have tried to hammer their favorite solution down the other party's throat. Communications break down. Positions harden. Disputes over facts and substance take precedent while the actual needs of both parties are unexpressed. There is no understanding of one another nor is there a search for middle ground to satisfy the needs of both parties.

The emotional side of the dispute has been ignored. Mediation insures that psychological needs, goals, and desires are expressed. In mediation, disputants are listened to, respected, save face, and emerge with their egos intact. They are in control over what happens to them. The process is open enough for people to really say what they want and what they believe. They also come to understand the bottom line issues the other party needs to resolve the dispute.

Expression is part of the healing. People can walk out with pride and self-esteem instead of feeling misused and discarded like they didn't matter. Respectful and equal communication softens the fear of being blamed or judged by the other party. A skilled mediator pulls out these needs and develops alternatives to meet as many needs of both parties as possible.

**Preparation for mediation.**

It is the farmer/rancher's best interest to come prepared with factual, realistic and documented figures. Help is available from farm management specialists, and ag financial counselors in analyzing the status and potential viability of their preparation. Financial statements, crop reports, loan information, fertilizers and other input costs should be accurate and realistic. The farmer needs to be prepared to defend his analysis and plan based on reasonable numbers and assumptions. This kind of preparation can't be done at the last minute.

The cost of foreclosure, realistic land appraisals, and fair market values are all useful so both sides can evaluate realistic debt restructuring alternatives to foreclosure and bankruptcy. This information is the way to judge whether the proposals are good or not. If the basic facts are disputed, then the mediation process gets bogged down from the start.

Mental preparation is important. It is important to establish goals in advance...and to work as a team. The spouse is required to be present. It is important to get a consensus in advance and speak as one mind. Sometimes, some pre-mediation work is necessary between husband and wife so they are unified on their goals.

The amount of preparation correlates with the success rate. Plans need to be presented with enthusiasm and in detail. Effective negotiating takes place when the problem and proposed solutions are described so well that the other party starts to believe it might work. To do that well takes knowing the other party's interests and finding a way to meet them while persuasively selling your own ideas.

**What does the mediator do?**

Trained mediators share many of the same techniques and perspectives. Mediation generally takes place in a neutral location such as a church, a library, or even in another town. The mediator explains the ground rules for mediation, the role of the mediator and what to expect. The authority, credibility, and control of the mediator create the atmosphere of trust and safety needed for frank and open discussions. Counsel may be present but the disputants are expected to take the lead in the discussions.

If the lender doesn't have authority from superiors to approve the agreement, the process of how the approval is obtained and by whom is discussed. The bargaining can go forward if good faith with the approval process is understood and built into the negotiations.

The facts are established during the first session about the legal interests or security at stake. If either party has a problem with the data, they are asked to clarify the issue or go back to their accountant, or if necessary, provide additional data.

Each party is allowed an uninterrupted period or time to state their feelings and points. The other party may write down questions and bring them up after the other party has finished. The mediator strives to maintain an atmosphere of courtesy and to keep discussions free of interruptions. It may be necessary to remind the parties of the ground rules for discussion from time to time.

The mediator may choose to use a blackboard or flipchart to keep track of key issues. The agenda is clarified and the parties agree on an order of talking about agenda items. This depersonalizes the problem and puts it "out there" where it can be seen. The issues are disputed, not the integrity or intelligence of the participants.

The mediator has two sets of skills. He or she must be effective at recognizing feelings and overcoming obstacles to communications. The second set of skills involves a problem-solving focus that sorts through issues and drives toward solutions.

The mediator asks questions, draws people out, gets them to explain themselves more precisely, clarifies points, reviews what they have said, orients the discussion, restates and rephrases offers, and reframes the points being made. Venting of emotion (within limits) is encouraged. The mediator acknowledges and legitimizes the feelings being expressed.

The mediator starts by trying to develop an understanding of what people want and need from the agreement before diving headlong into technical disputes. The key to mediation is getting everything on the table including the extenuating circumstances, and dealing with all of the issues forthrightly.

The mediator can call a recess and visit with one or both parties confidentially to calm a situation or to coach a participant on communication or negotiating tactics. Something is going on that doesn't meet the eye, the mediator can use the meeting to clarify an issue in private instead of confronting the party in the mediation session. Attempts at hidden agendas or covering up are detected and dealt with in a private and face-saving caucus.

The mediator may coach an angry or bitter disputant on how to detoxify their speech or reframe their position without unnecessary incendiary remarks. A mediator might suggest a proposal and test for consensus with each party. A recess may just be a breathing space to allow everyone to calm down. The parties in the dispute also have the right to ask for a recess or request a private meeting with the mediator.

If a deadlock is occurring, the mediator smokes it out. Hard questions are asked such as "Why can't you live up to that? or "What can you do? The mediator does what it takes to prod the process along while remaining fair and impartial.

A mediator listens for options and skillfully draws people out by his or her questions to consider new possibilities. The goal is to create an atmosphere where the parties themselves generate their own solutions through brainstorming an open-minded consideration of alternatives.

Attorneys, by virtue of their training, tend to give legalistic and advocacy advice while ignoring the psychological interests of their clients. An attorney can be most helpful by taking a passive stance during mediation and allowing their client to think and work toward solutions.

The mediator helps develop a non-binding memorandum of understanding between the parties. This should be reviewed and put into acceptable legal language by the respective attorneys.

Seventy to 80 percent of mediations are successful. That record is remarkable considering the history that brought them to this point, the high stakes and the emotions involved.

**Problems in mediation.**

Do you know any farmers that procrastinate? They come unprepared to mediate. Mediators and others close to this process believe many farmers could strike better deals by actively and positively approaching mediation as an opportunity. If one of the parties isn't negotiating in good faith, this will be obvious. The mediator will suspend mediation until the effort is genuine and a degree of openness is possible.

Most mediation fails because of stubbornness, pride, grief, or vindictiveness. Some people are too angry to see what is in their best interest. They want the other party to pay even if some of the pain is at their own expense. In these kinds of disputes, "hatred" is not a too mild of word.

Rigid "pie-in-the-sky" solutions not based on realistic facts don't fly. Disputants have to be flexible enough to identify what is realistic and still meets some of the other party's needs. Farmers, ages 40-60, may feel they have limited options. Their anger and feelings of despair may interfere with a problem-solving frame of mind.

Even with as much good will as can be generated, sometimes the numbers just don't add up and legal recourse is the only way. A bankruptcy or foreclosure is necessary to dissolve the relationship and relieve the parties from ongoing financial entanglements.

Some people are angry and negative. Way down deep they want to quit farming anyway but won't take full responsibility for making the decision. They want to drag it out and make others suffer along with them. The only way they can accept getting out of farming is to have it taken from them. They aren't looking for solutions.

All in all, mediation is a valuable process for all but a small minority of cases. The success rate is good and the process is a much more human approach than slugging it out through the courts. It is worth a try.

# Was It Fair?

Suppose a superior in your organization is going to rule on a grievance you have filed. Which of the following do you think determines how you will feel about the outcome?

(a) If the ruling is in your favor.

(b) If you are able to maintain indirect control by your ability to influence the authority figure.

(c) If the authority figure treats you with courtesy, dignity, and respect.

(d) If the procedures used to arrive at the decision are fair and equitable and that you had ample opportunity to present your evidence.

The answers are "c" and "d".

**Justice depends on the process.** Tom Tyler, a psychologist at the University of California at Berkeley, cites two studies. The first study of convicted felons showed they judged their experience with the court system primarily on whether they were treated fairly and not by the sentence they received. In a related study conducted by the Rand Corporation, civil litigants were willing to accept decisions by an arbitrator if they felt the procedures by which the decisions were made were fair.

In both of these cases, those affected by the judicial process didn't become more negative toward the authority figure even if the decision went against them. On the other hand, if they regarded the procedures as unfair, people who experienced an unfavorable judgment became bitter and negative toward both the authority figure and the system he or she represented.

Tyler surveyed the reactions of people involved with disputes about their feelings of justice following decisions rendered by judges, police officers and managerial supervisors. He found that acceptance of decisions by third party authorities occurred when the authority figure:

- treated them with dignity and respect, and affirmed their feelings of self-worth as a person with standing in the community.
- was perceived to be kind and showed concern for the well-being of all parties.
- was seen as being neutral, unbiased, honest, reasonable, and basing his or her decision on facts.

People experience justice when they feel that the procedures are fair and even-handed and when they feel the authority figure is respectful and unbiased in their interactions with them. These factors of "respect", "trust", and "neutrality" had independent effects on how people felt about their experience with authority.

Why should the way the authority figure relates to the disputant carry so much weight?

**Affirmation of self-worth.** When people themselves have an occasion in their lives to be subject to third party rulings, they hope, trust and fully expect that the process will be fair and just. The relationship between the disputant and the authority figure becomes a test of the social bond and trust the individual places in society. "Does this representative of society regard me as a person of worth?" "When it comes to my interests, will the system be fair?" "Will I get a fair hearing of my evidence?"

If people have a bad experience with an authority figure, the disillusionment can be profound. It challenges their basic assumptions that life is good and just and that people can be trusted. People hold on to their bitterness longer based on how they perceived themselves to be treated rather than the adverse nature of the actual decision. For the disputant, the issue of right and wrong gets muddied up with their feeling that their dignity is on the line.

**What does this mean?** Here are some implications for third party authorities who hear disputes:

* Attitudes of neutrality, openness along with with fair procedures lead to acceptance and compliance with decisions. People need ample opportunity to present their evidence. When people sense politics, back room deals, conflict of interest, prejudice, or other hidden agendas, they feel violated.

* Basic human relationship skills such as making eye contact, giving attention, showing empathic concern, listening, and extending common courtesies communicate respect and dignity to the individuals involved. Non-verbal facial expressions, tone of voice, body posture and social consideration communicate the attitude of the authority figure about the worth of the individual in the vulnerable position.

* The experience should be as interactive as possible. Mediation is a satisfying tool for resolving disputes because it maximizes the opportunity for discussion between the authority figure and the disputants.

Plea bargaining in criminal matters represents a respectful

way of including a defendant in a dialogue with the prosecutor and the judge. Decisions reached behind closed doors - conferences in chambers, settlement agreements etc. - outside of the presence of the affected parties weaken trust in the process.

When it comes to justice, the facts matter. So does winning and losing. But the hidden factor is how people feel about how they are treated by the authority figure and whether the process is fair. There is a lesson here for other authorities not wearing judicial robes or police uniforms, - parents, teachers, administrators, supervisors, government officials, church leaders, etc.

The quality of your relationships with people makes legitimate the authority you exercise. Abuse of authority upsets and enrages people. Power should be exercised with kindness, even-handed concern, patience, respect and consideration.

# How To Stop Thinking Like A Victim

Our society is fast becoming a collection of victims. Even "angry white males" have joined women, Blacks, disabled, farmers, the poor, Mothers Against Drunk Drivers, co-dependents, Adult Children of Alcoholics, gays and lesbians, physicians, government employees, teachers, truck drivers, veterans and every other conceivable lobby group, religious or ethnic minority under the sun. Fill in the blank for your favorite grievance and discriminated group.

**Strategies for dealing with problems.** So how do people act in responsible ways toward their problems without blaming or making excuses for themselves? The following four models show different ways of defining problems and how to arrive at a solution. Each model has its strength, arena of effectiveness and dangers.

**1.** *Seeing oneself as responsible for the problem and responsible for the solution.* This perspective benefits those who have resources and use them. They value independence. They believe in pulling yourself up by one's own bootstraps. They value helpers who can link them to resources, consultants, instructors, educators, motivational materials, exhortation and self-help. They expect themselves to strive, work hard, and expect their peers to do likewise.

Defeat or failure is blamed on oneself and might be experienced as catastrophic. It is hard to justify seeking help from others when they see themselves as responsible for their own solution. They can be too hard on themselves and too lonely.

**2.** *Seeing others as responsible for the problem and oneself as responsible for the solution.* This perspective benefits those who see themselves as deprived and have to fight against structural or cultural barriers to inequality. They are legitimate minorities who seek to redress an abuse of power. Their basic strategy is to collaborate with one another, assert and empower themselves, mobilize for action and rely on subordinates to broaden their base of influence.

They value interdependence, pressure, persuasion and organized group effort. They appreciate advocates and catalysts. In the role of helpers, they benefit the most. They can take full credit for bringing about a solution even though someone else caused the problem. The danger is in adopting a permanent negative, paranoid or hostile view of life and becoming alienated from the larger society.

**3.** *Seeing oneself as the source of the problem and others as responsible for the solution.* This perspective benefits those who feel guilty and need to depend on a group for basic structure and support. They feel helpless to overcome their personal difficulty and find help by submitting to external authority figures. Authority figures stress the importance of group affiliation as a source of power and safety.

The feeling of affiliation and belonging to a group of people with similar problems gives them strength and discipline to deal with their own problem. They value discipline in the group. They appreciate caring helpers who help them understand and cope with problems on an ongoing basis. The danger is reconstructing one's life around obsessions, dependency on group membership and support and becoming fanatical about the group cause. They are vulnerable to abuse of power within their own group.

**4. *Not seeing oneself as the source of the problem and seeing others as responsible for the solution.*** This perspective benefits those who do not feel directly responsible for the problem, yet feel incapacitated, mystified or helpless to provide a solution to the problem. They are not hard on themselves. Their problem temporarily exempts them from their regular responsibilities.

Experts are needed to help them define the problem and prescribe the correct treatment. The expert helps him or her identify alternative solutions and encourages problem-solving. The expert is a dependable source of ongoing help. The danger is dependency on the expert and a loss of self-reliance and abilities to deal with problems in the long term.

**Victim mentality.** What is the difference between belonging to an organized group that enhances our identity and power versus adopting a victim mentality that hinders our well-being?

According to psychologist Rebecca Curtis of Adelphi University, it is when we use our minority status to define ourselves as powerless and see others as "bad" people who abuse power. We make unfavorable comparisons between our "virtuous and deprived" status and others who have "undeserved" advantages and rewards.

These so-called advantages and abuse of power may really exist. What is destructive is a mentality of hopelessness and low expectations, a giving up or resignation in the face of such perceived unfairness. People who think like victims choose to suffer and take on a suffering mentality which may include anger, bitterness, depression, hurt, worry, helplessness and hopelessness.

This kind of thinking promotes low expectations, low performance and poor self reward. Often victims have a curious combination of low self-esteem and complacency. Victim thinking leads to a self-fulfilling prophecy. People adopt self-handicapping attitudes, screw up in other areas of their life and give their inherent power to others.

True victims need a caring, belonging, support, soothing, understanding and a period of nourishment to the point where they can mobilize their own energies, accept the loss or deprivation and move forward in a positive way. Sometimes a sense of anger and injustice is necessary to create a needed change.

The difference between being a victim and having a victim mentality is to not let anger and hostility permeate one's being and take away hope, enjoyment and power to act for oneself. A victim needs to take steps to get power or control in his or her life. It is an essential ingredient of happiness.

*CHAPTER SIX*

# GOING FOR HELP, HELPING OTHERS

## What Are The Facts About Suicide

The background for this information on suicide came from David Jobes, associate professor of psychology at Catholic University, Washington D.C., and Harold Elliot, police chaplain and author of, "Ripples of Suicide."

In 1997, suicide in the United States claimed 30,535 lives. It was the eighth ranking cause of all deaths. Homicide ranked 13th.

Suicide is the 3rd ranking cause of death among the young. In 1997, those over 65 made up 12.7 percent of the population but committed 18.8 percent of the suicides. Those 15 to 24 years old represented 13.7 percent of the population and committed 13.7 percent of the suicides. There are 4.1 male completions for each female completion.

Ten to 20 percent mean to die while 80 percent or more are ambivalent about death and are choosing suicide as one way of solving a problem. Seventy percent of victims give verbal and nonverbal cues prior to committing suicide.

**How many people actually kill themselves when attempting suicide?** An estimated 765,000 people attempt suicide annually in the United States. There are 25 attempts for every one completed. When it comes to attempts to complete suicides among young people, the ratio is 100-200:1 while the number of attempts to completed suicides is 4:1 for the elderly. There are 3 female attempts for each male attempt. An estimated 5 million living Americans have attempted to kill themselves.

Of all people who attempt suicide, only 10 percent complete suicide. However of all people who complete suicide, 45 percent had previously attempted suicide.

Twenty percent of teenagers have actively thought about suicide. Seventy five percent of all teen suicides involve drugs or alcohol. In the past 25 years, the suicide rate among teens has increased by more than 50 percent.

**How many people are directly affected by a family member or friend who commits suicide?** Each suicide affects at least six other people. Based on the 742,000 suicides between 1972 and 1997, there are 4.51 million survivors of suicide. In 1997, this represents 1 in every 59 people. The number of survivors of suicide grows by more than 180,000 each year.

**How prominently do firearms play in suicide?** Firearms account for 57.5 percent of all suicidal deaths. The percentage rises to 61.8 percent among the young and 70 percent among the old.

**What are the main signs of suicidal behavior?** The main factors are, 1) intolerable psychological pain, 2) extreme external pressures that frustrate important psychological needs, 3) a high degree of emotional distress or agitation, 4) a loss of hope, and 5) a negative assessment of self and one's ability to help change the situation. The most common purpose in suicide is to seek a solution to escape emotional pain.

What are the mental health issues connected with suicide? Mood disorders (depression and bipolar depression), substance abuse disorders (alcohol is involved in 40 percent of all suicides), presence of two or more disorders, learning disabilities, and schizophrenia and borderline personality disorders.

Behavioral issues include social withdrawal and isolation, acting out, or underachievement. As depression deepens, thinking becomes more black and white, rigid, and constricted - a refusal to think about alternatives.

**What should you do if someone is depressed and despairing about life?**

- Be yourself. Say what is natural for you. There are no formulas, just safe guidelines.
- Get them to trust you to tell you what is going on in their mind. Your words won't matter as much as projecting genuine concern through your body language and tone of voice. Talk as an equal. Don't come on with a lot of advice.
- Be calm and understanding. Be willing to hear and accept feelings. Don't interrupt their flow of thought. Show interest without giving the third degree.
- Ask simple, direct questions. "What happened?" versus probing, complicated questions. Steer them toward the pain instead of away from it.
- Don't side with the people who he or she is hurting or who may be hurting him or her. Let your friend struggle for his or her own answers even if you think your solution is obvious. When you don't know what to say, say nothing. Being silent is OK.
- Find out who in their support system is a source of strength and connect him or her with that person.
- Assess specificity and lethality of their suicidal plan. Have they thought about how and when they would do it? Do they have the means available? The more specific and well thought out the plan, the more dangerous the intent. Take away their access to the means they have of killing themselves.

**What shouldn't you do?** Don't ignore suicidal threats. Take all threats or attempts seriously. Don't keep it a secret. Don't promise confidentiality.

**Besides listening and referring, what is helpful to despair-**

**ing individuals?** Most people don't want to kill themselves. They want to end their pain. Communication helps bring relief. They have thought through their reasons for dying. They need help in verbalizing their reasons for living. Explore both sides.

The frankness and matter-of-factness about the discussion will help them engage their thinking and problem-solving abilities. Use your bond with them to form an alliance. Come up with a specific plan for the next few days and get them to commit to following the plan.

# When You Suspect Suicidal Thoughts

Suicidal thoughts are a common symptom of depression. Most teenagers or young adults have had passing thoughts of suicide. People confronted and overwhelmed with a major loss or tragedy may wish to escape their terrible pain.

With some exceptions, those who commit suicide and those who weather the storms and misery of life share this motive. *They did not or do not want to die.* The attractiveness of suicide lies in the promise of relief from overwhelming feelings of anguish, alienation, guilt, loneliness, frustration, anger, grief, and confusion - an intolerable situation from which there seems to be only one escape.

But there are avenues of escape from this inner storm of emotional turmoil and pain. One of the surest is the passage of time. Feeling or being suicidal is temporary. For the vast majority of people there may be a few minutes, a few hours or a few days when their despair makes them acutely suicidal. Acting out on a suicidal thought during such a state of despair is a tragedy - a permanent solution to a temporary problem.

With the passage of time, the emotional pain recedes, circumstances change, hope returns and the will to live comes back. However, during that critical time of acute despair, the suicidal person needs support and care. Co-workers, friends and family who sense the threat can take steps to help bridge the time until hope and the will to live return.

**What to do?** It is a frightening experience and responsibility to be in this position. How can they overcome their own fears and feelings of inadequacy to confront this delicate and painful subject? What is the right thing to say? What is the wrong thing? How can they be helped? Here are a few guidelines for intervening in the life of a suicidal person.

- **Be calm.** The suicidal person will best respond to an authoritative person who projects a sense of strength and control coupled with care and concern. Be accepting and communicate that he or she is a special, worthwhile human being.

- **Be a good listener.** Try to pinpoint the causes of the suicidal thinking and feelings. Help him or her identify and express their pain and hurt. Don't argue or debate the philosophical/religious reasons for living. Don't lecture. Don't try to talk him or her out of suicide. Don't argue. Don't analyze motives. Just listen.

- **Don't dismiss or undervalue what is being said.** Don't be shocked by what you hear. Don't stress the pain or embarrassment a suicide would cause the family. Don't offer "cheap" reassurance that things will be better. Don't promise confidentiality.

- **Ask open-ended questions.** Draw the suicidal person out. Get him or her to think. In verbalizing thoughts, the suicidal person begins to gain a sense of control over their emotions. "What are you doing now about your situation?" "What have you done?" "How did that work out?" "Who might be helpful to you?"

- **Ask specifically about suicidal plans.** Mentally note how specific the plans are. Assess the lethality of the method and the availability of the means. The more specific the plans, the more lethal and available the means, the greater the risk of suicide.

- **Be available.** Share your willingness to be available to talk and listen. Don't overpromise something you can't deliver. Be honest and realistic about your schedule.
- **Explore resources.** Find out whom the suicidal person might be willing to talk to about their situation - a priest or minister, a family doctor, mental health professional, or a special friend. If you are aware of community resources, mention the various sources of counseling available in the community. Your own experiences are especially helpful in making a "word-of-mouth" referral.

If you suspect immediate danger, take him or her to a hospital or involve law enforcement. Don't leave the suicidal person alone. Isolation, both physical and emotional, poses the biggest risk for suicide. If you are satisfied that the danger is not immediate, then connecting him or her with professional treatment will suffice.

- **Do something concrete.** Set a time to talk again. Arrange for an appointment or a next meeting. Get him or her to agree to a course of action and commit to it. Give a specific time for the next meeting or appointment. Insist on their compliance. Your voice of authority and willingness to assume control is welcome.
- **Obtain the help of others.** Don't carry this burden alone. Involve as many people as possible. Share your plans for getting others involved in this situation. Follow through with the plans you make and see to it that additional help happens. Mobilize and surround the suicidal person with their own support system of family and friends. Once the suicidal risk is out in the open, he or she will experience relief as the avenues of support open up.

Helping a person with suicidal thoughts doesn't have to be a big mystery. The biggest obstacle is having the courage to ask the hard questions. Once you have broken through and get the suicidal person to talk and share their burden, the process of recovery has already begun. Listen. Keep them talking. Take control. Make plans. Marshall support.

Even the fiercest storms are temporary. This inner storm, like all storms, is temporary. This storm, however, is not a storm to be endured alone.

# Help Is Available For Depression

Do our moods come and go without any control on our part? Thank heaven that is not true. We can do something to manage our moods and stress and even our susceptibility to depression.

Lynn Rehm, a psychologist at the University of Houston, emphasizes that depression is treatable. There are effective drug treatments and counseling techniques to deal with depression that are inexpensive and don't take forever.

He believes depression is caused when the connection between a person's behavior and their long term goals is broken. A depressed person sees the pathways to their goal either blocked by daunting circumstances or they have lost confidence in their ability to deal with the challenges presented by circumstances.

**Watch for distortions in thinking.** Without a belief or hope that they can accomplish long term goals, several thinking traps create or maintain a depressed mood.

A depressed person:

- pays selective attention to negative events and consequences in their life. Depression undermines their accuracy for predicting future positive events and overemphasizes the negative.

- pays attention to immediate consequences instead of their long term goal.

- resists changing their perfectionistic standards and goals. They are not flexible enough to either redefine their long term goals or consider alternative pathways to their goals. They believe their future efforts will be futile. Feelings of anger and hostility may accompany the depressed mood when there is a feeling of lack of control.
- takes excessive blame and responsibility for negative life events. They place the cause of failure or anticipated failure primarily on personal deficiencies. They are self-critical, unsatisfied and unaccepting of themselves. A depressed person also fails to take credit for the positive things that they are doing.
- engages in self-punishment and negative self-talk.
- gives insufficient self-rewards, especially rewarding small steps on pathways toward long term goals.

**There are ways to help.** Rehm's treatment consists of some structured teaching units that address the faulty thinking of a depressed person.

People are helped to clarify and think through their long term goals. They are coached on how to increase positive events on a day-to-day basis. They are shown how to pay attention to positive events, take pleasure and satisfaction in their long term efforts, be careful about assigning blame for negative events and how to take credit for positive events. They are also encouraged to take small steps toward long term goals and reward themselves for their successes.

**Looking out for Bi-polar disorder.** Psychologist Stephen Josephson of Cornell University Medical Center feels there is a need for careful diagnosis between depression and bi-polar depression.

Bi-polar depression is a biologic form of depression where a person alternates between a depressed mood and an excited or euphoric mood. In their manic state, they often go without sleep, have racing thoughts, pressured speech, become argumentative and engage in impulsive behaviors such as spending sprees, excessive drinking, gambling or sexually acting out. In extreme forms, their ideas may become grandiose and irrational.

This form of depression runs in families and has a strong genetic component. Medication can easily control it though certain kinds of antidepressants might trigger a hypomanic episode - hence the need for careful diagnosis.

Both Rehm and Josephson see value in psychotherapy for bi-polar disorder - besides taking medication. Rehm sees bi-polar episodes as being triggered by stressful events. Coping skills that help them better handle stress and their moods will make them less susceptible to recurrent depression or manic episodes. They also need to be taught how to monitor their moods and activities and to regulate themselves accordingly.

Josephson feels it is important for bi-polar patients to understand the connection between their reduced amount of sleep and how it triggers manic behavior. Leading a balanced life with exercise, work and play will lead to regulated sleep and fewer interpersonal conflicts. They can be trained in anger management so they can monitor their own internal cues. People are also coached on how to respond positively to others who might also provide helpful insight into their pumped-up moods. They need to learn how to get back to their regular routine.

Medication compliance is essential. Weight loss may trigger increased activity levels. Josephson also feels the moods of bi-polar patients are sensitive to light and dark in much the same way as Seasonal Affective Disorder, a disorder in which certain people become depressed from lack of sunlight during the winter.

# Going To A Counselor Is Hard But Helpful

**Why go?** People experience disturbing feelings such as depressed moods, uncontrollable fears, heightened anxiety, or low self-esteem. The problem may lie in a lack of control over behavior such as too much alcohol or drug use, overeating, losing one's temper or a persistent inability to relax.

It may be a problem in an important relationship. Tensions, anger, lack of understanding, too many unfulfilled expectations, disagreements and differences surface between a couple. It may be about concerns over children, job-related stress, or continuing problems such as headaches, chronic pain or hypertension that do not respond to medical treatment.

The problem itself may not be clear and the solution isn't easy. People do their best but feel frustrated when problems persist.

In these cases, the important and sensible thing to do is to get help. It is not an easy step. People don't generally involve outsiders with these kinds of difficulties unless there is considerable distress and unhappiness and until they have tried everything else. Just because it is hard to do doesn't make it any less sensible.

Heroic self-suffiency can become just plain stupidity. It takes sound judgment to know when additional help is needed and courage to ask for it. People don't like to ask for help with their own responsibilities unless it is truly needed.

**Is going for help a sign of weakness?** If people knew how different and growth stimulating counseling can be, they would be a lot less hesitant about seeking help. The seriousness and genuineness of the difficulties and the motivation of clients seeking help make counseling successful. A counseling relationship cannot be manufactured out of nothing nor can it be prolonged when the need no longer exists.

People who seek help are special. By seeking help, they demonstrate the desire to improve the quality for their lives and a willingness to pay the price to accomplish this. They are true enough to their goals not to let pride or even stigma prevent them from getting the help they know they need.

They go because they are highly motivated to change and humble enough to recognize the value of ideas originating outside of themselves. They are honest and willing to face themselves and their problems with no punches pulled. They want to develop their inner resources and coping abilities. Going for help is a sign of strength.

**Where do I go?** When an automobile breaks down, what action do we take? We take it to someone who knows what to do and can get us going again just as soon as possible. We do it even if it means admitting we made some mistakes or that we can't fix everything. We trust the mechanic's expertise and his or her definition of what's wrong and how to correct it.

We don't give up responsibility though. We usually have a rough idea of what the problem is and what will or won't work. The diagnosis of the problem and proposed solution has to be explained to our satisfaction before we agree to the proposed repairs. If the expert's ideas are badly inconsistent with our opinion, we trust our judgment and turn to someone else.

**Who do I see?** With human problems, there is a wide range of people who may, in fact, "know what is wrong" and are able to get the job done. The helper may be a family member, relative, friend, family doctor, mental health professional, or a minister or priest. Our belief in the credibility of the helper is a major factor in counseling success. Trust is a significant factor in willingness to follow through with their suggestions.

**What is counseling like?** Counseling is a special type of teaching in which the relationship itself plays a role in the learning process. It embraces a curious mixture of both love and separateness, freedom and authority, relating and teaching, acceptance and accountability, independence and direction, and support and confrontation.

Counseling is temporary yet powerful, caring yet objective. It is an experience in elemental honesty, openness, and courage. There is no room for falseness and pretense. It is also difficult and can be unpleasant. Growth is sometimes painful. Truth is hard to face. The old ways are hard to give up. To be open to change is a big risk.

The counselor takes time to listen and understand the client's views and values, gives hope and relief, redefines the problem, helps identify alternatives, teaches and models new skills, expects commitment, insists on follow through and monitors results. Competence and control are not undermined but enhanced.The responsiblity for working through the solution is left in the hands of the client - as is the credit for the change.

# Soothing Helps Trauma Victims

These ideas of soothing trauma victims are taken from the work of psychologist Elise A. Brandi of Harvard University.

Soothe: to bring comfort, solace, reassurance, peace, composure and relief. Even saying the word "soooothe" tells you it is something special.

Soothing has a long history. Mothers and fathers do this for their babies. A mother provides the protection a child needs when its own resources are exhausted. When her child is hyper-aroused and over-stimulated, a mother steps in to calm, soothe and lower arousal.

When this protection doesn't occur, a pattern of protest (an increase of adrenalin) and despair (a depletion of adrenalin) sets in. The same thing happens to a trauma victim.

The usual coping skill of a trauma victim is overwhelmed by an uncontrollable, terrible life event. During the protest phase, a trauma victim may experience panic, aggressiveness, irritability, nightmares and possibly an intrusive reliving of the trauma. The emotions are primitive, intense and overpowering. The victim feels helpless and incapacitated.

The stage of protest/despair is triggered by events that resemble the initial trauma. Emotional reactions can be triggered by a victim's own thoughts or everyday occurrences. Victims often show all-or-nothing responses even to minor stress.

It may seem strange, but trauma victims sometimes try to calm themselves by re-exposing themselves to trauma to release natural body opioids that have tranquilizing or calming effects.

More often though, victims compulsively use illicit drugs, alcohol, eating or exercise to calm themselves. To ward off anxiety, a trauma victim may try to seal their unwanted emotions and, memories from their conscious awareness. This takes a great deal of psychic energy and fragments their sense of self. Perhaps the most subtle and devastating effect is not the original trauma but the lack of caring and support after a traumatic experience.

Studies have shown that when a victim is left alone with a traumatic experience, without comfort and calming, the trauma remains unintegrated and injurious. The victim fails to moderate their emotions and they sense a loss of control. Failure to comfort a victim has a long term impact on their functioning.

The current trauma may also trigger heightened stress reactions in victims who have unresolved abandonment or trauma issues from their past. They were left alone and it has already had an impact.

**How to help a trauma victim.** The first step is to help the victim understand the physical and psychological aftereffects of trauma. The effects need to be identified in the victim's own situation. Helping the victim to know that their reactions are normal and expected helps him or her regain a sense of control and esteem. Victims need to be reminded of their history of effective coping and that the trauma they went through would overwhelm anybody.

Often victims feel guilty about their symptoms. They feel they should be able to fix themselves. Trauma victims need to know that recovery from trauma is not something they can do alone. Victims need relationships of trust; someone to challenge their irrational beliefs about themselves, someone to support their healthy functioning and someone to be emotionally available to them to offer them safety and comfort. This is similar to how a mother would respond to her child's upsetting experience.

**Soothing trauma victims.** Victims should be encouraged to soothe themselves in ways they know work for them. But more important than self-soothing is soothing by others. You can soothe by:

- creating an atmosphere that is calm and free of distractions;
- providing warm liquids - not stimulants such as coffee;
- encouraging exercise that releases natural body opioids;
- providing fluffy comforters, pillows, baths, showers and special foods;
- giving something personal to help them feel less alone;
- relieving them of important responsibilities;
- touching, embracing or massaging - if you are a spouse, parent, relative or good friend;
- going out of your way to meet little needs;
- encouraging experiences with nature and music;

Your soothing tells them that they are not alone, that they are cared for and worthy of love. It reaffirms faith at a time when they need it the most. Soothing is a gift - in a time of great need, a priceless gift.

# Helping Farm Families In Crisis

If a rural family suffers a calamity, illness or injury; rural neighbors are quick to pitch in with comfort, material aid and emotional support. It is one of the aspects of rural life that people appreciate.

However, there are few traditions for helping a suffering family who is in the process of losing a farm or ranch. Here the territory is a little less clear. How do you reach out to those families weighed down by onerous adverse circumstances? Here are some points to consider.

**Give love and acceptance.** The family often feels alone and isolated in their struggle and grief. Their faith and trust in others has been challenged. Even close relationships with friends and relatives suffer during this time of pain and turmoil. Proud and self-reliant people who aren't used to having strong emotional needs often erect barriers between themselves and the people who care about them.

These hard-pressed families may not feel comfortable in sharing feelings or knowing how to ask for help. Some may feel suspicious and untrusting of the things that have happened to them. It takes persistence and consistency for the power of love and concern to break through hardened shells. Physical presence alone at sensitive times is enough to send a strong message of support.

The attitude of family members (parents, siblings, in-laws, children and especially a spouse) and good friends mean so much as the family draws into itself. Support and acceptance by the people closest to them is a Godsend in troubled times.

Their own self–esteem may be floundering. Though they know deep in their hearts that they did everything right, they wonder how they are perceived in the eyes of others. Gospel and negative judgments weigh heavily on their minds and erode the faith they once enjoyed and took for granted about the goodwill of others.

**Little things help.** During a time of grief, people in trouble have little energy left over to deal with the troublesome ordinary problems that come up. Getting help with these tasks frees them up to deal with the more painful tasks in front of them.

Friends and neighbors can be sensitive to when a bag of groceries, a plate of cookies, an errand, a loan of a piece of machinery, or other gesture of support may fill a need. The aid probably is a drop in the bucket compared to the financial straits they are in, but small things affirm love. Small acts of kindness and thoughtfulness are truly large because they show the struggling family that people do care.

**Encourage communication.** Grieving people need to express and accept their emotions. Pain, fear, anxiety, depression, guilt, anger, and frustration are natural feelings under the circumstances. When pain is expressed, its hold is weakened.

Being able to talk about their troubles helps grieving people take control of their thoughts and emotions. It helps them define their feelings and their dilemma. By verbalizing their problems they also begin a process of considering alternatives. What is needed is a good listener. They need to trust that their innermost thoughts and feelings will be held confidential.

**Give material information, technical support and material aid.** People in the process of trying to stay afloat need to know about the path they are on. Some of the best advice given to a farm family in trouble comes from people who have been through the crisis already. They can share a message of hope and concern because they have been there.

It takes incredible love and strength to share one's loss in order to help someone else. They know what was helpful or not helpful to them. They've learned some things, even mistakes they made, that would be helpful to another family.

**What is extremely helpful is having access to good financial and legal advice.** Open and frank discussion about options and alternatives help most in the long run. There are tax and legal consequences to debt problems and the whole array of choices needs to be explained. For instance, if a farm family is leaving farming, the tax consequences need to be spread over two or three years instead of just one year.

Referring a struggling family to someone who can shed light on the practical dimensions of their problem may be the best help people can receive. This includes putting people in touch with those who can offer emotional and counseling support about communications and relationships.

Many of the unsung heroes are the ag business suppliers, lenders, creditors, and main street merchants who understand and work with people and their financial problems. Many of these business neighbors alter terms of repayment and carry these families at considerable financial risk to their own businesses. Whether the farm family survives on the farm or not, they will remember with great affection those people who put themselves on the line and made their path a bit easier.

**Financial aid from other family members is important.** The family is the first line of defense when the bottom falls out. These loving acts of sacrifice bind the family closer together.

No one person can or should fill all these roles. Each person in a rural community can play a part in softening the trials of these families as they are facing the loss of their lifestyle, their goals and dreams, and their equity.

# Helping Others Find Meaning In Crisis

The winter of 1996-97 wrought hardship, suffering and financial loss. Livestock producers in the Northern Plains had a devastating winter coming on top of low cattle prices. A killer spring blizzard capped off a winter of blizzards. Many people experienced fatigue, exhaustion and mind-numbing confusion from fighting the elements - the rising waters or the deep snows. It felt like being in a war zone.

Unprecedented flooding displaced families from their homes. Some farmland was too wet to plant. The assumptions of a normal, predictable, safe and secure life were shattered. Life was no longer manageable. These traumatic events challenged basic spiritual understandings of a kind, benevolent and just world. In many ways, farmers and ranchers who went through that winter were like trauma victims.

Psychologist Richard Tedeschi at the University of North Carolina at Charlotte has studied positive and negative effects of trauma and some of the challenges victims of trauma have to master:

- One must do and not do. Taking action is necessary to manage difficulties, but the tolerance of inaction, waiting and accepting is also important.
- One must learn to rely on others, but working out a crisis is up to the individual.
- Trauma is in the past and one must learn how to keep it there. On the other hand, it is more easily resolved if they integrate it into present life in some constructive fashion.
- One must be able to give up attempts at "primary control," such as attempts to reverse the effects of the trauma, where such reversal is clearly impossible. Eventually the affected individual must have a *willingness to accept* some aspects of the situation as unchangeable.

Tedeschi realizes these emotional tasks are paradoxical but make sense to those who go through them. Traumatic events have great power to transform or change lives in significant ways. It is highly emotional learning. With time, most of it will be for the good. Some of it may be for the worse. There are no short cuts. People have to go through it to understand the experience.

So how do family, friends and helping professionals help in situations like these? He offers the following advice.

- **Be respectful of an individual's processes of coping.** People respond to crisis in idiosyncratic ways. Positive change cannot be forced. It has to be experienced.
- **Be tolerant and accepting of ideas and rationales that are not completely logical.** Some positive illusions are beneficial in the coping process. Ruminations are helpful in trying to make sense out of the world. The greater the level and breadth of the ruminations that occur, especially in the time soon after the event, the greater the likelihood of positive integration of the crisis into that person's life.
- **Focus on listening rather than trying to solve anything for the person in crisis.** People in crisis need to verbalize

their feelings and conceptualize the problem. Offering a listening ear is the best immediate help you can give.

- **Take your cues from the victim's attempts to find meaning in the crisis.** Helpful advice and perspectives on growth and benefits from a crisis are not welcome immediately after a traumatic event. Timing is everything. Reinforce reasonable positive interpretations the individual makes. Specific solutions will be resisted until the victim feels understood and is a partner in the process.

- **Reframe or bring into sharper focus the changes that have occurred because of the crisis.** Be clear in your views that any benefits that come from the traumatic event are a result of the struggle with the trauma, not from any loss or change that might have occurred.

- **Strike a balance between accepting what is a normal response of pain and distress and communicating hope and encouragement.** People need to have their distress acknowledged. They also need hope. We either live in hope or we live in despair. After listening and empathizing with the painful reality, the trauma victim needs to be given encouragement and hope.

- **Be willing to engage in a religious dialogue.** Many people utilize their religious belief in trying to assimilate a life crises. Welcome these kinds of discussions and be willing to wrestle with ambiguity and the complexity of their confusion. Be accepting of their reassessment of religious beliefs, spiritual self-assessment and existential questions that arise from the crisis.

- **Encourage the setting of new goals.** Even small goals require self-discipline and persistence during recovery. Taking responsibility for helping oneself through personal effort is vital to managing their new life.

- **Encourage interactions with others who have suffered similar circumstances.** Loneliness and isolation are prevented along with the feeling that they are alone with their tragedy. Contact with those who are further along in their coping enables the victim to feel understood and to see positive problem-solving approaches to difficulties.

- **With time, the victim can seek out opportunities to be useful to others and gain purpose, meaning and strength that comes with helping others.** A pathway out of despair is to become involved in service to others, particularly to those less fortunate than oneself. Making comparisons to those less fortunate puts problems perspective and distracts the victim from his or her own difficulties.

- **Help the victim tell the story of their trauma and how it has affected him or her.** Healing comes with telling and re-telling the story of the trauma and the place it occupies in their life. Writing one's feelings is also helpful.

With retelling and with time, new perspectives will emerge. People will come to terms with the losses that have occurred, the existential lessons learned, the limitations they experience and the new possibilities in their lives.

Join your suffering friend in their journey of pain - in *their* way and at *their* pace. There will be a time when you might be on that path and others will help you make sense of what has happened to you. This is something we can do for each other.

## CHAPTER SEVEN

# TRANSITIONS OUT OF FARMING

# Out Of Bad Can Come Good

The debt crisis in agriculture of the mid-80s was followed by the drought of 1988 and by the flood and rains of 1993. For many farmers it felt like more than they could handle.

For farmers unable to plant, they knew by midsummer of 1993 that they wouldn't have a crop in the fall. Others, like the wheat farmers of northwestern Minnesota, thought they had a bumper crop only to discover within two weeks of harvest that it was worthless. Their whole year's work was down the drain.

To qualify for disaster payments, they had to burn their fields. The emotions surrounding that event were strong. It was like burning a piece of their heart. Farmers can rebound from one bad year. However, this isn't the only bad year.

I've talked with farmers who have been worn down by several years of high stress and low yields. Because of the high financial risks, one farmer said he dreads putting seeds in the ground in the spring and experiences relief when the harvest is in.

Suppose he, and others like him, leaves agriculture? What will happen? How will he and his family adjust? Research at North Dakota State University shows that over 80 percent of the state's displaced farm crisis families have made successful life transitions.

That isn't too bad for a profession so fraught with attachment and loss issues as farming.

**All's well that ends well.** It is hard to judge an experience as bad until we know how things work out in the end. It is through hard experience we grow. This isn't just a glib statement. In a study completed at the University of North Carolina at Charlotte, psychologist Richard Tedeschi and his colleagues investigated the kinds of personal changes that occur in people challenged by traumatic events.

They were compared to the changes in people who experience positive life events. Those who had been through a major trauma experienced more positive change in their lives than those who had a major success or achievement. They experienced an increase in their sense of humor, became more self-reliant, had more appreciation of things they took for granted and developed a greater ability to understand others.

**Growth through adversity.** The two groups didn't differ in their assumptions about life or in their religious beliefs, of participation. The researchers concluded that people develop greater personal strength, find greater depth of meaning and appreciate life more by going through major difficulties.

It's not a message we like to hear. We wouldn't wish a catastrophe on ourselves. We don't want hard experiences to test the resilience of our children.

If the experience turns out well, we grudgingly have to admit we like the changes it caused. I've heard people talk about their growth after having gone through a major trauma. They say they wouldn't go back to the way it was. They have changed. They are better human beings. They understand life differently now.

The knowledge and qualities gained through adversity have come at a tremendous cost. Their experiences made them who they are. Many people attribute their major successes to so-called failure experiences. Out of the ashes of defeat came the creative ideas that became the foundation of later success.

*"Failure is often God's own tool for carving some of the finest outlines in the character of his children; and even in this life, bitter and crushing failures have often in them the germs of new and quite unimagined happiness."* - I. Hodgkin

**Overcoming trials.** A noted researcher on grieving has found that many people express their grief through their creativity. Creativity is a channel for pain and insights that follow a loss. In one study of 400 eminent 20th century individuals, three-quarters had troubled beginnings.

Many eminent creative persons have dealt with early adversities including troubled childhoods, poverty, parental illness, traumatic loss or physical disability. The courageous processing of a traumatic experience serves not only to help resolve the loss but helps create an openness and flexibility that may not have been there before.

Progress involves overcoming difficulties. But these must be first seen, named and accepted as part of reality. Stress can be faced, made concrete and less frightening and then manipulated creatively.

Stress can be and often is a good thing. Good can come from bad.

# A New, Better Life

When do farmers involve outsiders in their struggle with an eroding financial position? When the pain is great enough. Even at that, the denial of reality may delay the decision to go for help and make a bad situation more precarious. Here are some reasons why turning to others for help is a smart thing to do.

**Find a 'safe place.'** A farmer needs to be able to verbalize his pain, grief and confusion in a safe place. The obvious place to begin is within the emotional closeness and security of the marital relationship.

This is a place where human beings can count on bedrock of love and acceptance. By expressing inner thoughts and feelings, a couple draws from each other the love and strength they need to deal with their situation.

Yet it is not that easy. Some men feel they must always be in control. They have come to believe that sharing confusion, fear and pain is not manly and is a sign of weakness. They take the financial survival of the farm squarely on their shoulders. They try to protect their wives from the harsh and painful reality.

By shielding their mate from reality, they deny themselves a check on the reasonableness of their own ideas and perceptions. In expressing how they feel about their problems, people define their feelings and gain control over their emotions. The problem takes shape and form. In conversing about a problem, people bring clarity to their thinking.

**Taking away fear.** Information about the problem takes away fear. Emotions keep the solution from happening. Advice from attorneys, accountants, ag financial counselors and farm couples who have been through similar difficulties gives profile to the problem. Once a farmer acquaints himself with the tools at his disposal, he puts himself in a better position to generate solutions. Adding information is like switching on a light in a dark room. It takes away the fear.

Having basic information brings back self-esteem. The farmer learns he is not the problem. The problem is externalized. He can be more logical. Now he is back on his familiar problem-solving turf. He can take action and do something to help his cause. The problem is no longer how the situation got out of hand, but what can be done about it now.

**Crossing hurdles.** Openness about problems opens the door to emotional support within the community. Letting others know about the financial problems is the biggest hurdle to cross.

Many farmers say this was the turning point in their recovery. They stopped worrying about what others thought and did whatever it took to survive.

One Kansas farmer described how he and his wife shared their hurt and pain first with a minister and finally from the pulpit in their church.

Once they made the first move, their neighbors and friends gave them overwhelming support. They gave their friends an opportunity to show their friendship. With the ice broken, they were able to be completely open and honest with others.

The pain of losing a farm taught them to care. They reached out to others for support and, in turn, supported others. The farm couple learned to value themselves independently of the financial problems. They realized that going from "blue chip" to "bad risk" wasn't so much a reflection on their management ability as it was about changing conditions.

This feeling of self-worth didn't come as long as they suffered silently and blamed themselves unmercifully for the problems. They became judges of their own character. They were no longer subject to the tyranny of public opinion, gossip or backbiting. They stopped measuring their self-worth by their net worth.

**A new, better life.** The financial crisis gave them new life - a better life. They didn't realize how restrictive it was to try to maintain their image in the community. By admitting their problems, they were free. With that freedom, they found the hope, honesty, growth and love that lessened their pain and enriched their lives. All in all, they wouldn't trade the changes that had occurred. Success can come out of failure.

Heroic self-sufficiency in certain circumstances is stupidity. Not going for help keeps anger and bitterness alive. Not going for help keeps people from understanding and loving one another.

A farmer doesn't need to be alone. By going for help, he heals himself through sharing feelings, pain and tears. He learns how much other people care. He rebuilds his self-esteem. He objectively evaluates his situation after seeking additional opinions.

By going for help soon enough, he improves his chances of working out his problems. Best of all, he discovers a new and better life, a more human and loving life.

If this is what getting help means, it can't be all bad. In asking for help, a farmer doesn't give up his basic responsibilities. What he is doing is expanding his resources to meet the problem.

# Life After Farming
# Can Have A Soft Landing

It is a tribute to human resiliency and coping that people can adjust their lives even after leaving a family farm. Eighty to 85 percent say they should have done it sooner.

The remaining 15 percent or so are the "walking wounded" from the 80s or from whatever era they left agriculture. It is likely that they are depressed, angry and fixated on their views that they were unjustly deprived of a life they loved.

Fortunately attrition from agriculture is more voluntary today. For many, farming is no longer enjoyable. It is too stressful, the hours are long, and the rewards and income are no longer sufficient. This is especially true for farmers on smaller, mid-size family farms with a conservative management style. A strategy of cost containment is no longer competitive with today's larger, technology-driven corporate farms.

This decision is not made easily. It takes several bad years in a row to get people to the point where they can leave a lifestyle, a profession they love and are good at and a community where they have strong affectionate bonds with friends, relatives and neighbors.

Stress in the family is a contributing factor. It becomes obvious that the farmer and/or his wife is unhappy. They see the effect on each other and the children. Off farm income has been added to the mix and still doesn't make a difference. People look at the prices they get for their products and the lack of control they have with their income. They don't see anything on the horizon that tells them its going to be any different.

The following letters capture the feeling many farm families

"Dear Dr. Farmer,

I have read your articles with interest for a long time. I now feel compelled to add some thoughts of my own. This letter is serving as a form of emotional release for me.

I am sure we weren't lazy or bad managers. Our production costs and output were always 'well above average' in our record-keeping group. We didn't spend money foolishly or play 'keep up with the neighbors.' I don't think it was anyone's fault. Weather, markets and interest rates moved in such a way that they created an impossible situation for us to make a profit.

We're having an auction to sell off our small line of older machinery. We'll rent out our farm and livestock facilities. We are leaving no unpaid debt. The lender is giving up a few months' interest, but otherwise is completely paid. We have no bills anywhere. With this as a background, I have a few thoughts I'd like to share with those involved and with those spectators in the process of a farm failure.

**First, to the debtor/farmer:**

Our problem was that the rain didn't fall and hog and grain prices did. Our input costs kept climbing. This year, hogs are still over $50, but we couldn't (or wouldn't) get back into production. Although $50 hogs is nice to see, we sold for that price in 1975. We even sold feeder pigs in 1975 for $60 a head. Input costs are a lot higher now. A 'good price' becomes a relative term. For us there was not enough equity to gamble while waiting for better times.

None of these things were our fault. We had no control over any of the factors leading to our failure. We decided to get out before we lost everything. The bank doesn't blame us and neither do we.

When we examined our lives, we found that our marriage, kids and lifestyle were all suffering because of a business we kept trying to salvage. 'Good times' will return to the farm. I know they will eventually. But in the meantime, the really important things in our life may have been sacrificed.

Pride is hard to swallow, but life is short. Business failure is painful, but personal failure can be devastating. I loved our business but my family and marriage come first. I'll gamble with money, but not with my family and home.

**Secondly, to the lenders:**

Don't assume we were dishonest or stupid. Also, don't be jerks. Last spring I was sick and in the hospital. The neighbors helped some with spring work. That was a very poor time to try to get my wife to sign a release that would allow you to take any assets needed to make our payment that was soon to be due. You didn't have to tell my wife you'd send the sheriff to get the payment.

I think you had your priorities screwed up. Your balance sheet and reports to the home office were more important than people you'd done business with for years. We even thought you were our friends. The whole thing ended well for both you and us. But no one treats my loved ones like that without arousing my Norwegian wrath. That wrath is slow to develop, but stays active for years.

**Finally, to the neighbors and other disinterested parties:**

Remember, failure isn't 'catchy.' Some folks have been enjoying our predicament. I suppose that's because our downfall must seem to make their position or status higher or more superior. If so, I feel really sorry for you. If one's success, contentment, and self-esteem is enhanced by another's misfortune, then that person is to be pitied more than the 'failure.'

Remember, I wasn't much competition. We never went on a big trip or vacation. We didn't even know what the current status symbols were.

I can, however, understand your jealousy. We have fun. We laugh, go for walks . . . we go on 'dates.' We enjoy the kids, even though (like most kids) they'll drive us nuts sometimes. We fight and make up. Eat your heart out. We're going to laugh a lot and soon.

After the auction, we're taking a few dollars and going away for the weekend. We'll soak in a hot tub, drink cheap wine and hold each other.

**To the vast majority of our friends and neighbors:**

Thank you for expressing your sorrow, offering your help in any way, and for your sympathy. We should have known you were priceless. I will be eternally grateful. I hope I can be that good a friend.

We'll get through this. All the really important things are just fine. Soon we'll feel the excitement of beginning a new chapter in our lives. And we'll remember the good parts of the chapter just ending. And all the good people." – An ex-farmer from Minnesota

This man and his family are going to make it. Wouldn't you agree? Hopefully each of us can respond to our hard challenges with such grace and hopefulness.

Dear Dr. Farmer,

I noticed you are having a retreat for farm couples so I thought I would write. We left farming and moved out here (Washington state) in 1989 when we were 50 years old. I want to second the notion that there is definitely life after farming – and a very nice life to boot.

What helped us the most was listening to experts like you and Dr. Harriet Light of North Dakota State University. I realized we had a choice. We could wallow in self-pity, become angry, etc. or we could decide to make a change in life. We came to the conclusion that farming was a business and that we had to make a business decision, not an emotional one. We have learned to love an urban area and enjoy many activities. We met new friends.

When people told me we wouldn't like it out here, I told them we planned to bloom where we were planted. To arrive in an area without a bad attitude would help us.

When our hospital went through some deep layoffs, I told my story and found it was helpful to others who thought they were too old to start over. Recently I responded to a story in our newspaper about a young farmer who committed suicide.

I truly wish it were different in agriculture. It's a shame that so many good, hardworking people have to leave farming. It has destroyed our small communities. But to be fair, farmers aren't the only ones who have had to leave their occupations and move elsewhere. We can argue until we are blue in the face that our country is making some bad decisions regarding agriculture which can come back and bite us, but in the meantime, farmers need to put food on their table.

Add my voice to tell farmers that there are other places to live and other people to meet in this world. Tell them to be flexible and open to other possibilities. After making a change, they may wonder what took them so long. We did. We learned that life can be beautiful in many settings. – a former farmer

For people who make this choice, there are opportunities and options. The non-farm economy cries out for skilled workers with common sense, a troubleshooting mentality and the rural work ethic. Farmers underestimate their skills and how they can fit into a non-farm economy. They need to explore their options and be open-minded about the fact that they already have a lot to offer.

There are also training and post-secondary education opportunities. Women with farming backgrounds thrive as non-traditional students and begin careers they always wanted to try.

People have to give up the moral and purposeful goal of their role as family farmers in feeding the nation and the world. They need to find a purpose to make their new work meaningful. This will take time. It may take two or three years to replace the love of agriculture with a new dream. There is usually a rough period of adjustment as ex-farmers work through their grief, get used to a town or city lifestyle and find a niche that suits them and offers creative challenge.

Meanwhile, living with neighbors "next door," lack of open spaces, no caring for animals, nervousness about raising children in town, and a dislike for traffic congestion are tough adjustments for these transplants.

For some ex-farmers the change in occupation has immediate benefits. They experience relief from the stress of big debts, a more reasonable workload, and more family time - home in the evenings, on weekends and real vacations. For many, getting out of agriculture opens up this world of family time and less pressured finances.

As one ex-farmer commented, "We have 'fun.' We laugh, go for walks. We go on 'dates.' We enjoy the kids. We laugh a lot. We are getting through this. All the really important things are just fine. We feel the excitement of beginning a new chapter in our lives. And we'll remember the good parts of the chapter just ending - and all the good people." This is a message of hope many farmers need to hear.

# Helping Farmers Make A Transition

The global economy creates opportunities and hardships. With technological advances in agriculture, the marketplace is highly competitive and favors high/volume, low/cost producers. This economic reality along with favorable growing conditions worldwide for the past few years has resulted in many basic food surpluses and consequently low prices.

Mid-size and small North American family farmers are reeling and looking at unfavorable forecasts. Policy-makers are concerned about how to help farmers stay in business. All the efforts to keep family farming alive need to be coupled with helping farmers make a transition out of agriculture. This is not throwing up a white flag of surrender to the forces working against family farming, but compassionate realism for the casualties of the global economy.

Here are some ideas on what is helpful to farmers in transition.

**- Information about resources.** Resources need to be set aside for training and higher education on a regional basis. Using regional resources as a base, innovative programs using a combination of "distance learning" technologies and commuting can help farmers retool their skills without disrupting their families.

Job and higher education fairs specifically targeted at farmers can help a farmer see the possibilities of a new career. Farmers need information about these particular resources and career opportunities to help them overcome their fears.

**- Support for family living.** There should be family living support to accompany any job training or higher education programs for ex-farmers. If farmers knew they could support their families during their efforts to establish new careers, they would access these programs with enthusiasm. Tuition waivers and other benefits that don't address family living fall short of what is needed.

**- Planned departure.** Farmers need information about taxes and the legal consequences of leaving agriculture. Off-farm work, selling or leasing a part of the land and retraining while still being on the farm makes a transition smoother. Preserving as much equity as you can also helps make any transition easier. Fighting too long and then being forced into a quick decision works against the farmer.

**- Finding hope.** "Life after farming" stories need to be told. They can and do connect with new careers that satisfy them and adjust to a new lifestyle.

For ex-farmers and their families, there is a predictable period of adjustment that will be painful. This transition period out of farming needs to be researched and explained to farmers who embark on this path.

**- Special support.** Ex-farmers need to be connected with other families who are in the same situation. Support groups are wonderful. There are ex-farmers who have made successful transitions who are willing to be mentors to new families leaving agriculture. Congregations and communities need to be alert to new families moving in and connect them with each other in small groups. Colleges and technical schools can provide specialized services, support, and networking to link former farmers together.

- **Addressing fears.** Myths about the depravity and dangers of city life need to be debunked. People can live good lives and can be just as happy in the city as they are in the country. A move or two during childhood can be beneficial to the development of self-confidence and social skills. Children adapt. It is the parents' fears that need to be overcome.

- **Going through it together.** Farmers and their families need positive communication and coping skills to help them support each other during a transition. Change is stressful and impacts each family member differently. Husbands and wives often reach the decision to leave on different timetables. There can be periods of estrangement and irritation when they have different goals and priorities.

Farm families can get help through counseling, retreats, and educational programs on stress management. Effective communication and mutual support are important keys to successful transitions.

- **Saying goodbye.** There is too much shame, hurt and bitterness connected with a silent exodus from the community. There is nothing to be ashamed of. The forces that dictate the transition are far beyond the farm gate and catch even the best in their sweep.

Churches, friends and caring communities can provide a non-judgmental atmosphere for the families who leave farming. Farewell parties, support during auctions and on moving day allows farm families to grieve and to say goodbye. The community also needs to acknowledge the loss, show that it cares, grieve and say goodbye. It makes healing easier.

Leaving farming doesn't mean failure. It means coming to the end of something and beginning something new. A transition. A caring society can help ease the way.

# Decision To Quit Agriculture Made Thoughtfully

**On a personal level, how does the current situation com-
pare with past years in agriculture? How tough is it?**

I've had farmers come to see me in the middle of the farming
season to discuss their personal coping, their overall goals, their
lifestyle and their decision to stay in the business. Others have come
about their marriage problems due to stress. And this is in the middle
of the summer [1998]. It hasn't happened quite like this before.

I get many letters and comments about the toll the ag economy
is taking on people's spirit. One choice is to leave agriculture on
one's own terms. Many are choosing to quit, not as a failure, but as a
business and lifestyle decision.

**What kind of farmers and ranchers are we talking about?**

I am talking about those in their late thirties, forties and early
fifties who have been successful in agriculture. They are at the top of
their ag careers. They are filled with doubt and worry about the future of agriculture.

They also have assets that they have worked hard to build.
Part of their decision is to leave early with something to show for
their efforts. This is different from the farm crisis years of the mid-
80s when farmers were forced off the land when they had nothing
left.

**That must be a tough decision - to leave agriculture when
they are capable producers?**

There is family heritage - land in a family name, personal
identity as farmers, being one's own boss, being attached to nature
and outdoor work, leaving a close community of family and friends.
That is the tip of the iceberg as far as the attachment rural families
feel.

Add to that the mixed feelings about seeing themselves, or
being seen by others, as a failure. They love rural life as a good place

to raise a family, have a fear of city life and worry about what else they can do with their life.

**When farmers and ranchers bring up the choice about quitting, what do you say to them?**

I remind them about how good they are at what they do. I tell them that their drive and work ethic will serve them well in society. Ex-farmers and ex-ranchers rise to the top in whatever setting they choose. I tell them that there will be a period of adjustment and that most families who leave agriculture are satisfied with their new lives within three or four years after they leave.

**What about their fears that family life outside of the country won't be as good?** It isn't all economics. Part of their decision to quit has to do with all the stress, worry and long hours - the rural lifestyle hasn't been good for them or for their marriages and family. They know that.

They don't like the direction agriculture is taking them in terms of pressure and workload. Then when the losses come in, it is defeating to the spirit.

I try to reassure them that life in the city is OK. Rural families carry a lot of myths about city life being dangerous and corrupting to children. Families can raise children well in cities and towns. Adjusting to traffic, congestion, having neighbors close by, and working for someone else will take time. Many will miss their animals and their privacy.

Many families experience relief from stress, the pleasure of an 8-hour day, a 40-hour work week, and a dependable paycheck. They like family vacations and a lifestyle that leaves time for each other.

**What about connecting with something as satisfying and challenging as the rural life? Isn't that a pretty big hole to fill?**

That is the hard part. People are leaving something they love and are good at. The three or four-year adjustment I talk about is the time it takes to connect with something new and work through their feelings of loss. These are multi-talented people who just need to experiment with some new or old dreams and ideas before they settle down.

**Does age limit them?** No. It isn't how old you are but how flexible you are. Each time we make a major shift in careers in our life, we start a new creative cycle for that career. Actually, changing careers keeps people young and vital.

**What kinds of jobs do they find?**

The sky is the limit. Many go back to college. Some look at professional careers. With disaster aid, there will be opportunities to get help. Many have skills that fit well in construction and skilled trades. Many choose jobs that keep them outdoors and working with agriculture in some fashion or another. Many start other businesses and continue to be self-employed.

They need to be patient and find that niche that will satisfy them. If they quit while they are ahead, that should give them even more options for trying different things. Most of us in society are just one or two generations off the land. We are descendants of parents or grandparents who successfully made this change.

# Moving? Don't Forget the Kids

If you are moving this year, you will be joining some 41 million other Americans including 6 million children. Everything changes. Everything is new. People. Work. Places. You lose the familiar. You are starting over.

You don't belong anymore. It will take effort to fit into your new location. Researchers say it takes six months to a year and a half to feel comfortable with a move. The feelings of loss, anxiety, anger, sadness, and fear are normal for parents *and* children.

Children who have moved 6 or more times are 77 percent more likely to have behavioral problems and 35 percent are more likely to have failed a grade. Sure, the types of families that move that often has something to do with it. However, getting used to new rules, teachers, expectations, curricula, friends and surroundings takes its own toll on children.

Denver clinical psychologist Thomas Olkowski has surveyed 2,500 elementary and middle school age children about their experiences with moving. He also has a clinical practice in which he works with families who are having difficulties adjusting to moves.

Olkowski has written a book, "Moving with Children: A Parent's Guide to Moving with Children." He outlines how a family move affects children and effective coping strategies for dealing with the move.

**How children react?** Children don't like to move. Their anger, resentment, sullenness, tantrums and resistance are normal. They can be excited one minute worried the next or even heartbroken the next. Happy-go-lucky kids suddenly become moody, insecure and apprehensive. Children in the same family are on different schedules with their emotions about the move. Sometimes they ignore the move and act like it won't happen.

Children want predictability in their lives. They worry about making new friends. They wonder about their new school. Will it be too hard? Or different? In addition they feel bad about losing their friends, their room, home and neighborhood.

Older teens especially resent a move. It disrupts their own quest for identity and separateness at a time when it is natural for them to be pulling away. They are giving up the social ties, jobs and activities that are a part of who they are.

**What can parents do?** Parents can ease the emotions by doing a few things, both before and after the move. The family can plan their move together and act as a team in creating successful adjustments.

They can explain their own feelings of loss and apprehension and normalize the experience for their children. They can explain why the move is necessary and engage in dialogue about it. They need to take time to listen to their children and let them air their complaints and feelings.

Children take their cues from their parent's attitudes and coping skills with the move. One common mistake though is to paint a too happy a picture.

Issues of loss need to be dealt with in addition to all the changes caused by the move. Counseling or support groups are extremely helpful.

**Tips for parents**

* Tell children early so they can make their own adjustments and say goodbyes properly. This will give others a chance to recognize they are leaving.

* Help them say goodbye to your house by encouraging them to plant a flower or leave a gift. They can leave a list of names and ages of the children in the neighborhood and describe what is special about the house or community.

* If realtors are showing the house, get the kids away while the "Looky-Lou's" are poking around.

* Involve children in the house hunting but only after you have narrowed your choices. They tend to fall in love with the first thing they see.

* Let the child assist in packing their own dearest possessions and let them choose the things they want to throw or give away.

* In your new location, set up the children's rooms first.

* Make the move in the summer. In the fall, they will start new with everybody else.

* Take the time to let them get to know their new neighborhood without having to cope with a new school and friends all at once. Go exploring together.

* Enroll them in activities so they can make friends before school starts. Meeting children at church will also give them a head start of fitting in.

* If you live close by, visit your old neighborhood and allow them to satisfy their curiosity.

* Let the teachers and counselors know that your child is new. If you are arriving after the school year has started, take the

time to learn the basic ground rules for classroom and school. Make sure introductions are made.

**Advice from children** Be yourself. Relax. Don't brag. Don't always talk about where you came from. Don't show off too much. Don't try to carry on the traditions and styles of your old community. Be friendly.

# From the Farm to College

North Dakota State University Extension Service invited a number of ex-farm couples to come and describe their experiences about leaving farming. I was a discussion leader for a table that discussed transitions and careers. Here are excerpts from one woman's perspective on what she learned and experienced about leaving the farm and going to college.

**What challenges of growth and change came about as a result of leaving the farm?**

I grew up on a farm and married a farmer. You do not see any other way of life. You don't dream of being something else. It just never enters your mind that you are going to someday be off the farm or doing something else.

I'm 44 and I think when I was 35 I didn't even know any of this was going to happen. Well, it happened. A decision as major as getting off the farm makes it so much harder. When we went to make the decision, I remembered telling a therapist years ago for another crisis we went through, "I feel like I am going to die if I make this decision. I feel like I'm going to die if I change. Or if I talk about this I'm going to die. You'll fall off a cliff." What she said is that you just have to move through it, don't stay right there, just keep moving through it.

And so then my husband and I one night were talking and we could no longer say, "Boy it just can't get any worse than this." We quit saying that and we talked about it and decided what would be the right thing to do. We would make the decision instead of the banker. That way we still have our self-esteem.

One time, I had been laid off at my place of employment. I know what it is like for them to make that decision. All it was was a part-time job and it just about killed me. It was real hard on me. I get a lump in my throat when I think of it because it wasn't my decision. I thought it meant something was wrong with me.

Ok, at that point we decided to get out of farming. We didn't know how or didn't talk about how. We didn't know who to go to, how to do this. What do you do? Who do you call on the phone? We didn't even know where to turn. And we knew that it was happening to people all over. But do we call them and ask them? Or do they think we are nuts for asking how do you get out?

That was the challenge, but when we made that decision, I had the best night of sleep I had for years. I'll never forget how good it felt to go to bed and have that huge dread off my shoulders. I don't know how my husband felt, but it was difficult for him.

I think really that I was the stronger one in this situation and I pulled him through it. And after he got through it he said, "Boy this is really nice." I was thankful I was able to pull him through it. I thought about farm wives and farm husbands who don't have a relationship and wonder how they survive. I can't imagine it.

**If you had no idea of another life, what helped you find out about another world out there?**

I didn't know that college was for me. I thought college was for people who were real, real, real smart. For people who knew every word in the dictionary. I really did. What I did was I decided to go to college. I went through all the stomach pain and terrible anxiety. My husband had to literally help me to the door to make that big step. All I did was make the decision and I did what that wonderful person said years ago to do - "just keep moving through it and don't stop." And I just kept moving through it.

**So some good advice is to do something and things will**

**start to fall into place later.**

Yes, just keep moving, keep going forward and make the decision and go through it. What happened is life outside of farming embraced me. I have really been helped tremendously. There is so much support out there. I thought it was really odd that at my age I would be going to school.

Everyone has been so happy for me. My biggest worry was I was too old to learn. I learned in sociology that our ability to learn peaks in our forties and doesn't even start to go down until we are in our 80s. When I heard that in class, I was thrilled. I was ready to learn now. So it has been fun ever since. It's just an open door and since then I've grown and changed a lot.

I know there is life after farming. But I do sadly look back on farming. I miss that life.

# What Good Is A Farm?

Recurrent wet weather years in the upper Midwest and tough economic conditions have put considerable pressure on small and mid-size family farm operations. Many farmers and ex-farmers from that era have commented on how my writing helped them think.

A farm woman describes the small foothold she and her family has made in starting again in farming after having lost their farm to Chapter Seven bankruptcy. They are now renting a tractor and several small parcels of land.

Reflecting on the emotional turmoil surrounding the loss of the farm, she made this comment. "We were guilty of feeling so strongly for our farm. Never again! It is only a business and a piece of property. If it doesn't 'pencil out,' get out."

That family learned a great lesson. To love something that much and then lose it is to endure great pain. In the end, they found that the farm was a means to an end - the generation of income to sustain a loving family and lifestyle - rather than an end in itself.

**Irrational attachment to the farm.** A farm, like a child or a business, can absorb attention, resources and energy. There is joy in watching it grow, improve and take on beauty.

A farm, especially one that has been in the family for generations, can be the object of great attachment and adoration. It assumes a mythical quality and a life of its own. "The farm must be kept in the family." Too many people have loved it, cared for it and sacrificed for it to allow it to pass on to unhallowed hands.

Some farmers, otherwise practical, rational men, develop an obsession with the farm to the point where they contemplate throwing away their lives as they anticipate its potential loss.

The love of a particular piece of ground or set of buildings is also the basis of father-son partnerships. This "love of the farm" promotes difficult and unnatural dependency relationships between adult males. Both father and son have difficulty sorting out the complexity of their relationship as they struggle to understand their mutual obligations.

The farm can also be the object of intense competition. Between siblings it can be a symbol of ultimate parental love. It can also be a source of power for parents to wield over children who would sacrifice their own integrity to gain possession of it. Off farm heirs can also maintain a passionate interest in the farm and have strong expectations regarding its care and disposition.

**Ownership of the farm.** Farmers derive status from ownership of land - or the pretense of ownership, as generally someone else holds the mortgage. To be an owner of land is to be somebody. That is greater than possessing wealth in other forms.

Many farmers accept drastic cuts in their standard of living to maintain their status as an owner of their operation. No matter how debt-ridden, they still have status among their peers as long as they retain "ownership."

**Where is the mistake in all this?** Why is ownership of a

farm so seductive? Why does it generate such irrational attachment? Some people make their homes the object of their lavish care. Others may be collectors of art, dishes, old cars, coins or guns. Some "love" their gardens, for others it is golf. Some may be excessively devoted to their work or to the National Football League. The list is endless. The love of a farm may be the highest and most socially acceptable form of this common human tendency.

These things are not necessarily bad unless they become ends in themselves. A little discontent keeps us moving, learning, reaching and producing. But to reach for more and more without real purpose or limit creates a discontent that cannot be satisfied.

Daniel Defoe said it best. *"All the good things of the world are no further good to us than they are of use; and of all we may heap up, we enjoy only so much as we can use, and no more."*

**Serve people, not the farm.** The farm is to serve people and not people to serve the farm. People are important. People are worthy of love. We can love people without limit. It is their growth and development that is important. The farm can help in that process.

**What good is a farm?** What good is a farm if it drains the family of emotional well-being, loving and fun times together, and is the source of worry, anxiety and heartache? What good is a farm if it drives a wedge between marriage partners and causes fights and arguments?

What good is a farm if the farmer devotes all his waking hours and energies to its service and neglects that which truly has life - his wife and children?

A farm is good if it does not become the object of unnatural affection. It has a use. If it stops being useful, of what value is it?

The pain and suffering of farm families financing huge debt problems is compounded by their undue affection for the farm. Perhaps the last and hardest lesson of the farm crisis of the 80s is the one mentioned by the farm woman.

"We were guilty of feeling so strongly for our farm. Never again!"

# Two Poems From The Heartland

In 1999 a farmer and a rancher shared their poems with me. I am using their poems with permission.

Loren Ingrebretsen farmed near Felton, Minnesota. He and his wife attended a retreat for farm couples leaving agriculture. He read this poem at the retreat.

### A TIME TO STOP
### by Loren R. Ingebretsen

In the recesses of my memory
In a place that is safe and warm,
Lives a boy, without any fears,
Playing, on the farm!

That boy grew up simply,
In an environment safe from harm.
Learning that work is a gift from God.
It was part of living, on the farm!

That last day before college,
With unknown fears to shield,
I needed time to think it out,
So, I drove a tractor to the field!

I met a girl so special,
And asked her to be my wife.
Together, we returned to the farm,
To give our children a start in life!

Twenty five years we toiled,
Our children: our finest crop.
And now with Ag prices so low,
We feel it is time to stop!

From the depths of my soul,
There is a terrible ache.
And yet, I know the time is right,
For the decision, we must make!

God calls to me from somewhere,
Saying, "I have kept you from harm."
'Don't you know, there's more than raising crops?'
"Living on the farm!"

So, we will rent out the land,
And take the hand of the One we know,
For He has always been with us,
Showing us where to go!

I understand more fully now,
That what kept me safe from harm,
Is that God was and is the firm foundation,
Of life on our farm!

Ron Tebow is a rancher from Moses Lake, Washington. He attended a stress management program for farmers, ranchers and orchardists in North Central Washington facing economic hardship. He recited this poem at the gathering.

## JUST A PEASANT
### by Ron Tebow

His lineage defined him a peasant
Never to receive a higher call.
A laborer is the service of the King
Counted least among them all.

But with diligence he approached his tasks,
His integrity was on the line.
He figured the endeavor to which he was attached

Was worthy of his time.

So without applause or recognition
He quietly completed the job that he'd began.
Drawn by the notion that his reward
Was in doing the best job he can.

He never saw his name in print,
No trophy or plaque he'd hang up on his wall,
But the epitaph inscribed on his tombstone read,
"He more than fulfilled his call."

Now I present you with this metaphor
A scenario that each one of us face.
An issue that invaded our lives individually
If we're counted in the human race.

I speak of the farmers and ranchers
Who've taken on the job of feedin' us all.
They stand as a lonely remnant
Gladly willin' ta answer their call.

They're not drawn by currency
Or the need to accumulate things.
Many times their only compensation is the smell of a fresh
    cut field of hay
Or the song that a Meadow Lark sings.

So I challenge you, the next time you sit down to a meal
And discover, by golly, there's food in front of you.
Consider the source of that alluring aroma
And give that peasant his due.

To order additional copies of
# *Honey, I Shrunk The Farm*
### please complete the following.

$16.95 each *(plus $3.50 shipping & handling)*

Please send me _____ additional books at $ _____ each

*Shipping and Handling costs for larger quantites available upon request.*

Bill my: ❏ VISA  ❏ MasterCard   Expires _____

Card # _____

Signature _____

Daytime Phone Number _____

**For credit card orders call 1-888-568-6329**

OR SEND THIS ORDER FORM TO:
**McCleery & Sons Publishing**
**PO Box 248**
**Gwinner, ND 58040-0248**

I am enclosing $_____
❏ Check  ❏ Money Order

Payable in US funds. No cash accepted.


**SHIP TO:**

Name_____

Mailing Address _____

City _____

State/Zip _____

Orders by check allow longer delivery time.
Money order and credit card orders will be shipped within 48 hours.
This offer is subject to change without notice.

### Charlie's Gold and Other Frontier Tales

Kamron's first collection of short stories gives you adventure tales about men and women of the west, made up of cowboys, Indians, and settlers.
Written by Kent Kamron. (174 pgs.)
$15.95 each in a 6x9" paperback.
(plus $3.50 shipping & handling)

### A Time For Justice

This second collection of Kamron's short stories takes off where the first volume left off, satisfying the reader's hunger for more tales of the wide praire.
Written by Kent Kamron. (182 pgs.)
$16.95 each in a 6x9" paperback.
(plus $3.50 shipping & handling)

### Bonanza Belle

In 1908, Carrie Amundson left her home to become employed on a bonanza farm. One tragedy after the other befell her and altered her life considerably and she found herself back on the farm.
Written by Elaine Ulness Swenson. (344 pgs.)
$15.95 each in a 6x8-1/4" paperback.
(plus $3.50 ea. shipping & handling)

### First The Dream

This story spans ninety years of Anna's life. She finds love, loses it, and finds in once again. A secret that Anna has kept is fully revealed at the end of her life.
Written by Elaine Ulness Swenson. (326 pgs.)
$15.95 each in a 6x8-1/4" paperback.
(plus $3.50 ea. shipping & handling)

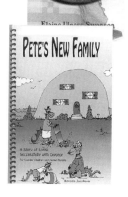

### Pete's New Family

Pete's New Family is a tale for children (ages 4-8) lovingly written to help youngsters understand events of divorce that they are powerless to change.
Written by Brenda Jacobson.
$9.95 each in a 5-1/2x8-1/2" paperback.
(plus $2.50 each shipping & handling) (price breaks after qty. of 10)

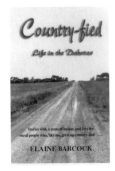

### Country-fied

Stories with a sense of humor and love for country and small town people who, like the author, grew up country-fied . . . Country-fied people grow up with a unique aware-ness of their dependence on the land. They live their lives with dignity, hard work, determination and the ability to laugh at themselves.
Written by Elaine Babcock. (184 pgs.)
$14.95 each in a 6x9" paperback.
(plus $3.50 in shipping & handling)

## COMING NOVEMBER 1st . . .

### It Really Happened Here!

Relive the days of farm-to-farm salesmen and hucksters, of ghost ships and locust plagues when you read Ethelyn Pearson's collection of strange but true tales. It captures the spirit of our ancestors in short, easy to read, colorful accounts that will have you yearning for more.
Written by Ethelyn Pearson. (160 plus pgs.)
$24.95 each in an 8-1/2x11" paperback.
(plus $3.50 in shipping & handling)

### Pay Dirt

An absorbing story reveals how a man with the courage to follow his dream found both gold and unexpected adventure and adversity in Interior Alaska, while learn-ing that human nature can be the most unpredictable of all.
Written by Otis Hahn & Alice Vollmar. (168 pgs.)
$15.95 each in a 6x9" paperback.
(plus $3.50 in shipping & handling)